THE CONCISE
VISITOR'S GUIDE TO
YOSEMITE

Although the author and publisher have made every effort to ensure the accuracy of the information in this book, neither party assumes any responsibility for errors, inaccuracies, or injuries resulting from partaking in the activities described herein or by taking the author's advice. It is strongly suggested that you talk with an expert, such as a park ranger, prior to engaging in outdoor activities in any national park.

Readers should be advised that websites, phone numbers, and other sources for further information may have changed or disappeared between the time this was written and when it is read.

ISBN: 1-4392-3429-9
EAN13: 9781439234297
LCCN: 2009902777

Visit www.booksurge.com to order additional copies.

THE CONCISE
VISITOR'S GUIDE TO
YOSEMITE

MATT BOLTON

This book is dedicated to the memory of my late father,
Ronald Kent Bolton,
who accompanied me to Yosemite on
our only father-son trip, in 1993.

TABLE OF CONTENTS

Acknowledgements   ix

Preface   xi

Introduction   xv

Chapter 1: How to Get to Yosemite   1

Chapter 2: My First Visit   3

Chapter 3: What Could a Typical Day at Yosemite Look Like?   7

Chapter 4: Where Will I Eat?   11

Chapter 5: Where Will I Sleep?   17

Chapter 6: Hiking Options   27

Chapter 7: I Don't Want or Like to Hike. What Else Can I Do?   51

Chapter 8: Tours   71

Chapter 9: Important Phone Numbers and Websites   77

Chapter 10: Why is a National Park Vacation Economical?   83

Chapter 11: Wildlife in Yosemite   85

Chapter 12: What to Do If You Only Have One, Two, or Three Days   91

Chapter 13: Activities Just For the Kids   95

Chapter 14: Weather, Winter & Snow Chain Requirements   97

Chapter 15: Wildfires   103

Chapter 16: Yosemite's Neighboring, Majestic National Parks   107

Chapter 17: Final Thoughts   111

Appendix A: Miscellaneous National Park Tips   113

Appendix B: Day Hiking Essentials   117

Index   121

ACKNOWLEDGEMENTS

I wish to express my thanks to the National Park Service and to Yosemite National Park for allowing me to use the maps in this book. I also want to acknowledge the NPS.gov website as an invaluable resource in gathering specifics on locations, times, contact information, and other specifics used in this book.

I'd also like to express my gratitude to Reineck & Reineck for graciously allowing me to use the Mariposa Grove map in chapter 6.

A heartfelt thanks goes out to my wife Karen for her resourcefulness and assistance. Without her, this book would have never gone from an idea to a published reality.

PREFACE

My name is Matt Bolton, and my passion is for our beloved national parks. I am not one of the lucky ones who gets to spend their entire life, day after day, year after year, visiting national parks. I have never been overseas to visit Europe or Australia. The only foreign country I have ever had the privilege to visit is Canada, and what a beautiful place our friends to the north have. However, my family and I have made it a goal to visit as many national parks as possible, and along the way, we have been fortunate to visit most of the United States' major national parks, as well as those of western Canada.

I have visited Yosemite National Park (NP), Kings Canyon NP, Sequoia NP, Muir Woods National Monument (NM), Cabrillo NM, Redwoods NP, and Point Reyes NM in California. I have visited Olympic NP, North Cascades NP, and Mount Rainier NP in Washington. I've been to Crater Lake NP and Oregon Caves NM in Oregon, as well as to both the north and south rims of the Grand Canyon in Arizona. I've been to Yellowstone NP and Grand Teton NP in Wyoming, as well as Zion NP, Bryce Canyon NP, Arches NP, and Canyonlands

NP in Utah. Other trips have included Rocky Mountain NP, Mesa Verde NP, and the Black Canyon of the Gunnison NM in Colorado, Denali NP and Kenai Fjords NP in Alaska, and Haleakala NP and the USS Arizona Memorial in Hawaii. I've hiked at Glacier NP in Montana, Mammoth Cave NP in Kentucky, Indiana Dunes National Lakeshore, Great Smoky Mountain NP in Tennessee and North Carolina, and Gettysburg National Military Park in Pennsylvania. I have driven through the Everglades NP in Florida (too many alligators to hike through the swamps there). Finally, my family and I have also traveled to Waterton International Peace Park, Jasper NP, Glacier NP, Yoho NP and Banff NP in western Canada. Most of these parks I have visited once, a few twice, but I have visited Yosemite NP five times.

This in no way makes me an expert. If you want an expert, talk to a park ranger at any of the parks. They've been trained, schooled, and tested. They are extremely knowledgeable, friendly, and willing to assist anyone. However, if you wish to locate some help in preparing your trip, if you are seeking an honest opinion and candid advice from someone who has vacationed at Yosemite many times, if you are feeling kind of overwhelmed and not sure where to even begin to prepare for your first trip to Yosemite, then I hope you find this book to be the answer. I hope you find it to be the right thing at the right time to get you feeling properly prepared and somewhat educated on this fantastic place. I have tried my very best in this book to give sage advice, coming from someone who simply loves Yosemite and has traveled to most all parts of the park, and on multiple visits.

The concept behind this book is for it to serve as a concise, reliable, and easy to use resource. I hope it will assist you with such needs as knowing where to get a meal, understanding why you might choose one day hike over another, knowing where to see Giant Sequoia trees if time does not allow you to visit all three groves, planning how to spend your evenings, knowing where you might safely swim and where you must not, knowing what to do if you encounter wildlife (and I hope you do), knowing how to see the sights by guided tour, making sure your kids have a great time as well, and much more.

Hopefully, you will get something out of this book that always makes me envious: a well planned and great trip to Yosemite.

INTRODUCTION

My wife encouraged me to write this; I have never written a book previously. The topic is, in my opinion, about the greatest single land asset of our beautiful United States: Yosemite National Park. This unbelievable, breathtaking piece of land remains undiscovered, unfamiliar, and never visited by the majority of people. To make an analogy: Just as all puppies are cute, but some are clearly cuter than others, and all desserts taste good, but some clearly taste better than others, all national parks are beautiful, yet some parks are far more beautiful than others.

My attempt here is to give advice and suggestions, to give tips from someone who has covered most all of this park, and on many visits. I am not trying to force my opinion on others; you can get books and brochures on Yosemite from a million different places. They are all good but give basically the same information. They tell you about accommodations, history and geology of the park, where places of interest are located, food options, admission fees, and distances and highlights of hiking trails. What is difficult to find is soundly based and well researched opinions regarding the many things to do, and from someone who did it the hard way.

I have made five trips to this fantastic place and never had anyone to advise me on what to see if I had limited time, where to stay, where to get the right food for a hike versus a well-earned, big dinner, or the many other tips that I have included here so that you can get it right the first time. You are probably a person thinking about your first trip to Yosemite. It seems beautiful and fascinating, yet at the same time, enormous and remote. You probably have a fair amount of apprehension as you try to figure out where to begin. Hopefully, the time you spend absorbing this publication will pay off in the form of a good trip, if not the very best trip of your life. I certainly hope so.

Yosemite is a place to be inspired, a place to exercise or relax, a place to stand beneath some of the tallest waterfalls in the world (specifically the fifth and seventh tallest, and the two tallest in the U.S.), a place to spend time among majestic wildlife, and a place to enjoy food, from fine dining to sub sandwiches. You can snow ski, ice skate, bike ride, ride horses, swim in a stream or lake (there are even multiple swimming pools), and much more. Yosemite is simply the greatest place I have ever been.

I will never forget my parents' visit to Yellowstone National Park. Upon their return, they told me that they saw Yellowstone and spent a grand total of two hours in the park. My parents are a prime example of good-meaning folks who, unfortunately, had no concept of what the national park experience is really all about. If you see yourself in this same mindset, then hopefully this publication will open your eyes to the offerings and beauty that is right there for the taking.

Yosemite is the third oldest national park, following Yellowstone and Sequoia, in a park system consisting of over three hundred locations. It includes groves of the largest living things in the world, Giant Sequoia Trees; an abundance of waterfalls, including two of the world's tallest, Yosemite Falls and Sentinel Falls; two breathtaking valleys, Yosemite and Hetch Hetchy; some of the country's greatest hiking; in most people's opinion, the greatest granite rock climbing at El Capitan; varying climates by regions, elevation, and time of year; and various wildlife, including black bears, mule deer, and coyotes. There are 747,956 acres, 1,169 square miles (about the size of Rhode Island), over 263 miles of road (195 paved), and 800 miles of hiking trails. Yet Yosemite remains 94 percent designated wilderness.

According to the National Park Service, Yosemite's operating budget for 2008 was $26,554,300, and the park is visited by more than 3.5 million people annually. The busiest period of the year for Yosemite is June through September, while the slowest month for visitors is January. A comprehensive study conducted in July of 2005 showed that 82 percent of Yosemite's visitors are from the United States, while the countries representing the most foreign visitors are England, France, Holland, and Japan. Forty-eight percent of visitors responded as first-time visitors. Yosemite is home to over 85 species of mammals and 150 different birds. Elevations within Yosemite range from 2,000 to 13,000 feet above sea level.

Yosemite's seclusion and relative isolation made it a known beauty to Native Americans, yet it remained undiscovered by Anglos until Captain Joseph Walker led an expedition over the Sierras in 1833. The first tourists are believed to have visited the Yosemite Valley area about 1855.

A group of visitors persuaded U.S. Senator John Conness to author a bill to protect the valley from development and exploitation. As a result, President Lincoln signed an act ceding the valley and Mariposa Grove to the state of California.

In 1868, conservationist John Muir made the first extensive study of the area and its geology. Muir was the first to postulate that the Yosemite Valley may have been formed by glacial erosion. Articles written by Muir discussing the possibilities of negative exploitation of the park persuaded Congress to declare the area surrounding the already state-protected valley and Mariposa Grove a national park, in 1890. In 1906, California returned its portion of the park (the valley and the Mariposa Grove) to the U.S. government. The nearly 1,200 square mile area became Yosemite National Park, much the same as we know it today.

In this book, I will attempt to give you the skinny on eating, places of interest, activities, preparation, expenses, hiking, wildlife (what to worry about and what not to worry about), basic accommodation advice, and how to open up the world of Yosemite. Even as a five-time visitor to this majestic place, I've only taken one solid bite out of all Yosemite has to offer.

Let me also put in a plug here for what an unbelievable bargain Yosemite, or any national park, is. The admission fee for Yosemite is $20. This gets you, your car, and as many people as you can fit into it twenty-four-hour access to Yosemite for a full week. Compare this to the cost of a movie for a family of four, not to mention that most movies these days are disappointing and last around ninety minutes. The national parks are the best value in family fun anywhere.

By the way, accommodations are a bargain as well. This is why they often book up to a year in advance. They do not charge what the market will bear or a fee based upon supply and demand. If they did, they would be far more expensive. They simply charge a bargain fee and let the early planners get them! (more on this fantastic bargain in Chapter 10)

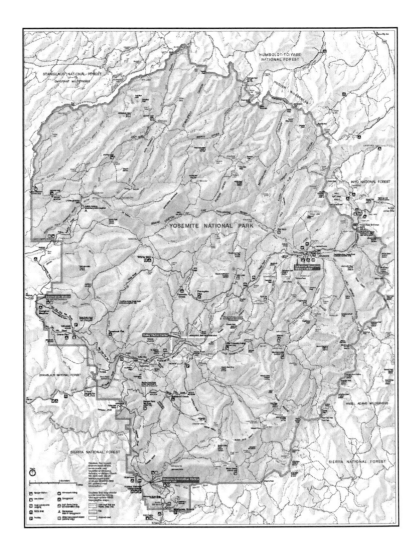

Chapter 1

HOW TO GET TO YOSEMITE

T here are two ways to get to Yosemite. You might live close enough to drive (in which case, I'll let you get out your atlas, as well as admit that I am jealous) or, if you live further away, you should fly to Fresno. Of course, you may find an unbelievably better priced flight to Tahoe, San Francisco, or Sacramento, and in that case, I'd take it. However, for most people, the most practical way to get to Yosemite is to fly to Fresno and rent a car. Fresno has a very nice and modern airport, served by several of the major airlines. It also offers car rentals, featuring most of the major car rental companies.

Yosemite is a very enjoyable two- to two and a half hour drive from the Fresno Airport. The drive is interesting, largely because it is constantly changing. As you drive out of the airport and through Fresno, it is flat and dry, often 100 degrees, plus. You'll probably feel like you are closer to Las Vegas and a desert vacation, rather than a few hours from the terrain, climate, and vegetation of Yosemite! As you drive northeast into the Sierra range, it gets much more wooded, increasingly hilly, and eventually mountainous.

It also gets much milder. As you leave the desert climate in Fresno, you will leave the palm trees behind and drive into the pine forests of the mountain terrain.

The town of Oakhurst is a charming town that can fulfill all of your needs prior to getting into the park. Oakhurst is about a half hour before the south gate to Yosemite National Park and offers groceries, lunch, gas, and really anything you might need. I do suggest visiting a grocery store and picking up snack foods and drinks for your time in the park. You will get better prices here than in the park itself. There are no chain grocery stores in the park.

While passing through Oakhurst, I suggest stopping by the Yosemite Sierra Visitors Bureau. This area visitor's center is staffed with friendly people who can assist you with all of your needs and questions, not only concerning Yosemite, but covering all towns and attractions in this part of California including Oakhurst, the Sierra National Forest and the Bass Lake area.

Chapter 2

MY FIRST VISIT

I readily admit that upon my first visit to Yosemite, actually my first real visit to any national park, I was unprepared for the experience. I had no idea what I needed to take along for a safe and enjoyable hike, or how much time would be needed to make it a productive visit. My wife and I planned a vacation to central and northern California, with time spent in San Francisco, Lake Tahoe, and a full two days planned to see all of Yosemite—or so we thought. We basically made sure we had a reservation for a place to stay, and we knew what route to take to get there. With that basically representing the breadth and depth of our planning, off we went.

We drove from the northeast entrance, the Tioga Pass entrance, to the valley and decided there was still plenty of time to begin a hike to the top of Upper Yosemite Falls. My wife and I, without seeking advice on this trail, set out late afternoon with just a moderate amount of drinking water on what is rated one of the most strenuous day hikes in Yosemite. We actually did complete the hike, but not without blisters from inappropriate footwear, a bad

3

case of elevation change sickness from basically running back down the trail, and a much needed stop with a good Samaritan who gave us a friendly lecture on hiking as well as his last PowerBar® so that we had enough energy to complete the hike.

On day two, we hastily crammed in as much as we could possibly see in a day and made sure we turned in early enough to be able to rise early again the next day and make the long drive to San Francisco for our flight home. We simultaneously came to the sickening realization that we had scheduled far too little time to see what had easily become the highlight of our entire vacation, and we wondered why we did not just spend the entire week of vacation at Yosemite. It reminded me of the times my father would drive the family from Indiana to Chicago to see a Cubs game. We often arrived by the middle of the second inning, and we always left by the top of the ninth to avoid getting caught in the mass exodus. I always felt like it was an awful lot of effort. I wondered why my dad never allocated sufficient time to get the most out of this great family event.

Anyway, my first time at Yosemite was a pivotal moment in my life. On this very short visit, I learned that I had never really understood the unbelievable enjoyment that the national parks had to offer. I knew I had a lot to learn, but at least I now realized that I had been missing something wonderful, and that it was right there inviting me to come and explore it further.

I knew lots of families who on every vacation went to yet another beach, amusement park, or ski resort. I wondered, *had I found my thing? Would the national park experience be my life's passion and the type of get-away vacation that, year after year, would bring unforgettable memories to my family*

and me? We committed right then and there that we would get educated on the park experience and return another day, properly prepared with supplies, proper attire, a well thought out agenda, and a sufficient time allotment.

Chapter 3

WHAT COULD A TYPICAL DAY AT YOSEMITE LOOK LIKE?

My ideal day at Yosemite, or any National Park for that matter, is built around hiking. Let me be clear though that there are many ways to enjoy Yosemite, even if you do not wish to hike or are not physically up to it. However, allow me here to describe my ideal day at Yosemite, which is usually built around the park's fantastic hiking trails!

There are numerous hikes that take you to see unbelievable natural beauty, including waterfalls and giant trees, which you have probably seen numerous times on calendars and wondered where the pictures were taken. Day hiking offers solitude, back country beauty, impromptu wildlife sightings, and exercise, allowing you to eat at your heart's content throughout your trip and still return home to stand on the scale and see that you actually lost weight on your vacation.

My family and I usually pick up breakfast items at one of the stores within the park or just outside the park. There are numerous stores at Yosemite to get basic groceries including Village Store, Badger Pass Sport Shop (winter only), Crane Flat Store, Curry Village Gift and Grocery, Camp Store at Housekeeping Camp, and Pioneer Gift and Grocery at Wawona. There are also grocery options at stores or hotels just outside the west entrance at El Portal, or the south entrance in the town of Fish Camp. More limited options are available just outside the northeast entrance in the town of Lee Vining. We usually pick up muffins, fruit, cereal, juice, and milk. This makes for a very economical breakfast, and more importantly, it is a big time saver. We can quickly eat while getting ready in our room, cabin, or tent, and hit the hiking trail much earlier than a formal restaurant breakfast will allow.

However, after breakfast, our next stop is for food again. Prior to hitting the trail, you must make sure you have more than enough food in your backpack (did I forget to mention that you will want to get a decent backpack) to satisfy lunch and snacking while on the trail. While we are on the subject of backpacks, I STRONGLY suggest getting a CamelBak®, or one of its competitors, where the pack includes a bladder scientifically designed to keep the water ice cold. My family and I all hike with these. I once spent five hours in the Grand Canyon at around 100 degrees, and when I finished my hike, I still had ice in my water. I hope it goes without saying that when you are thirsty or simply drinking regularly to keep yourself hydrated, there is a big difference in the quenched thirst factor between drinking ice cold water and drinking warm water! It is well worth the expense. Backpacks of this type will cost you roughly $50 to $90.

I will tell you here that my favorite moments from any national park trip are the lunches on the trail. Don't knock it until you experience it! To find a flat rock to sit on and lay out your sub sandwich, chips, trail mix, etc. while enjoying a pristine view along the trail is as good as life gets! Anyway, you do not have to be a health freak when planning food for the backpack, just be sure you place a mix of items, including some that are healthy and provide quick energy. I always get a sub sandwich, fruit (apple, banana, or raisins), and a PowerBar®. However, I also might include a big cookie, Fig Newton's®, or potato chips; after all, you do want to enjoy yourself on vacation right? Also, while you should pack at least 150 percent of as much food and water as you think you'll need, it also does not hurt to take along a soft drink. I usually drink only water while on the trail, but I enjoy a soft drink while stopped for lunch. Also, remember to take all your trash with you. This is what the signs that read, "Pack it in, pack it out" mean.

As far as picking a trail, it isn't hard. However, picking the right trail is very important, both for your enjoyment and your safety. You do not want to hike beyond your limits. You can get hiking books on the entire park for a nominal charge at the souvenir shops, at your local chain bookstore, or through the internet. You can get free hiking maps published for various sections of the park through the internet, as well as at any visitor center, along with sage and up to the minute advice from a park ranger. You will want to pick a trail that has the degree of difficulty that's appropriate, scenic offerings that appeal to you, and a time estimate that fits your time allocation. In other words, be smart. If you have never hiked before, start with an easy or moderate hike. Also, if the time estimate is say, four to six hours, start in the morning, not at 4:00 pm. Be sure to be aware of and inquire about bear sightings. No need to panic here; just be sure to read Chapter 11!

Build your way up to tougher trails. You might try an easy trail on day one, a moderate trail on day two, take a break from hiking on day three, and then if you have yet to really push or challenge yourself, try a strenuous hike on day four. On my most recent visit, I tackled the famous Half Dome Hike. This is a seventeen-mile hike, taking ten to twelve hours, and includes 400 feet up a 60 degree slope at the very end to summit at the top of Half Dome. It is referred to in many publications as the greatest day hike in North America. It was one of the best days of my entire life, but not the type of thing to try if you are brand new to national park hiking—or seriously afraid of heights. Also, remember to avoid trails and especially high unprotected and exposed rock, like Half Dome, if lightning is predicted or in the area.

Anyway, a day hike for me usually ends in mid to late afternoon. While hiking provides an unbelievably satisfying feeling of accomplishment for me, it leaves me more than ready to enjoy a hearty dinner, ranger lecture, and an early bed time, because the next day, I begin the cycle once again.

CHAPTER 4

WHERE WILL I EAT?

Yosemite offers a surprising number of options for meal time. Most any option is available, from casual and economical dining in the valley at the Food Court (strange name choice for the cafeteria at the Yosemite Lodge at the Falls), where you can get an unbelievably large plate of tasty spaghetti for around $5, to a fine dinner of steak, fish, pasta, or chicken at The Mountain Room Restaurant at the Yosemite Lodge at the Falls. There's also truly fine dining at the Ahwahnee Hotel. Other options in the heart of the valley are Degnan's Café (coffees, smoothies, and baked goods), Degnan's Deli (again, a great choice for the early morning replenishing of the backpack), a pizza place above Degnan's Deli called Degnan's Loft, the Village Grill (burgers, fries, and milkshakes), buffet style meals at the Curry Pavilion, the Curry Village Coffee & Ice Cream Corner, the Curry Village Pizza Deck & Bar, the Yosemite Lodge Cone Stand at the swimming pool, and the Happy Isles Snack Stand. In addition, there's the Mountain Room Lounge at the Yosemite Lodge at the Falls. This is basically a bar/lounge, but they have some snacks, light sandwiches, and appetizers available, and a big screen to watch a ballgame.

Options outside of the valley include a couple of choices at the Wawona Hotel, plus a weekly Wawona Hotel Lawn Barbeque. These options include the Wawona Hotel Dining Room and the sandwich shop at the Golf Pro Shop. Additionally, there is the Tuolumne Meadows Lodge, the Tuolumne Meadows Grill (boy, do the burgers cooked outdoors here and eaten under a tree looking out across the high country on a long summer day taste great), a limited seating restaurant at The White Wolf Lodge, the Glacier Point Snack Stand, and the Sliders Grab-N-Go in the day lodge at Badger Pass, during winter operations.

Snacks, ready-to-eat sandwiches, and various hiking and energy-type food items can be acquired at the Curry Village Gift and Grocery, the Crane Flat Store & Gas Station, as well as the Wawona Pioneer Market.

Let's get down to specifics on some select options, starting at the high end. The finest dining in the valley and the entire park is the award-winning dining room located in the Ahwahnee Hotel. The Ahwahnee dining room features chandeliers and fine china, plus a great view. The dining room is on the north side of the hotel, tucked in against and looking up at the north wall of the Yosemite Valley. Dinner reservations are highly suggested, especially during the summer months, and can be made by calling 209-372-1489. They have a dinner dress code that they refer to as "resort casual." They used to require jackets for men at dinner. Upon my most recent visit, they relaxed it to collared shirts and long pants for men; dresses, skirts/slacks and blouses, or evening pants suits for women.

I strongly suggest the following: My family and I always eat a breakfast or lunch at the Ahwahnee. They are served in the same historic dining room, but the meals cost much less, the restaurant is less crowded, and they require only a casual dress code. It not only saves money, but because of the relaxed dress code, it is much easier to pack for the trip, especially if traveling by air. The dinner menu features such main dishes as Prime Rib, Chicken, Trout, Lamb, and Duck. Lunch is the usual burger, club sandwich, soup, and salad options. The Ahwahnee also features special menus for select holidays such as Thanksgiving and Valentine's Day. The dining room hours are 7:00 – 10:00 am for breakfast, 11:30 am – 3:00 pm for lunch, and 5:30 – 9:00 pm for dinner.

Taking a slight step down in "fanciness," along with a comparable step down in cost, the next finest dining would be either the Mountain Room Restaurant at the Yosemite Lodge at the Falls or the Wawona Dining Room. We'll first stay in the valley and briefly discuss the Mountain Room Restaurant. This dining room also features great views like the Ahwahnee, as it is also against the north wall of the valley, and offers a very relaxing décor. Cocktails and appetizers are available, and the food is quite good. Dinner options include steaks, seafood, and pasta. There is the option of patio seating during the warmer months. Like the Ahwahnee, it is open all year, but is run on a first-come basis, taking reservations only for parties of eight or more. Reservations for such parties can be made by calling 209-372-1274. The restaurant is open 12:00 noon – 11:00 pm.

The Wawona Hotel Dining Room (located not in the valley, but near the southern end of the park, approximately thirty miles and an hour drive from the valley) serves breakfast, lunch, and dinner, and has excellent food as well. The menu here features more standard or traditional dishes for dinner, including pot roast and trout. Award-wining turkey chili is offered on the lunch menu. Also offered are western outdoor barbeques on Saturday summer evenings and a great brunch on Sundays. The hotel and its dining room are officially closed during the colder months, yet open select weekends during this period; call first if in doubt. Dinner reservations can be made by calling 209-375-1425.

Curry Village is the largest lodging property at Yosemite. It is located in the heart of the valley and offers many dining options. The Curry Village Pavilion offers all-you-can-eat breakfast and dinner buffets. Here you can enjoy salads, tacos, pasta, chicken, beef, and varied desserts. The Pavilion is usually open late March through sometime in October. There is also a Pizza Deck (guess what the menu is here), the Curry Bar, with a food menu of burgers, salads, pulled pork, and more; the Taqueria, serving Mexican cuisine; and The Ski Buffet, a flat priced, very filling buffet, plus dancing (on just a few select winter dates), to cap off a full day of skiing at Badger Pass.

White Wolf Lodge serves box lunches to go and serves sit-down dinners. Reservations for dinner are required and can be made by calling 209-372-8416. The Tuolumne Meadows Lodge sells box lunches as well and offers sit-down breakfasts and dinners. Reservations are also required here and can be made by calling 209-372-8413.

Many of the smaller eating establishments discussed here that are located in the valley, plus all of the options mentioned outside of the valley, are seasonal and not open in the winter months. However, you can count on the Food Court (again, a cafeteria), the Mountain Room, and the Ahwahnee Dining Room, all located in the Yosemite Valley, to be open year-round.

Ahwahnee Hotel Dining Room

Chapter 5

WHERE WILL I SLEEP?

Another great thing about Yosemite is that accommodations are varied and sufficient in number, but only available if you plan ahead. National Parks are not the type of place where you pull into town and start looking for the local Holiday Inn®. If you plan a year in advance or at least six to eight months, you will have a much more enjoyable park experience.

Within the park are tent cabins (with central shower facilities and scattered bathroom locations), the rustic and well used Yosemite Lodge, historic rooms at the Wawona Hotel, and the expensive, fine lodging at the four-diamond Ahwahnee Hotel. Specifically, you can choose from tent cabins, cabins with bath, and cottages at Curry Village; canvas topped three-sided cabins with community baths and showers at Housekeeping Camp in the valley; tents with community baths at the Tuolumne Meadows Lodge; or regular cabins and tent cabins at the White Wolf Lodge on Tioga Road. There are nice, yet aged historic rooms at the Wawona Hotel or standard rooms at the Yosemite Lodge at the Falls in the heart of the valley. The finest and most expensive accommodations are the 99 hotel rooms in the main building or the twenty-four stand alone one-bedroom cottages at the Ahwahnee Hotel. Be sure to at least walk through and see the Ahwahnee hotel. Again, consider breakfast or lunch there without the strict dinner dress code. One final park lodging option is a cottage resort called The Redwoods, near Wawona, just six miles from the south gate.

I will add one BIG PIECE OF ADVICE here: If you book on too short of a notice that you cannot get the overnight accommodations you desire, do not give up. My wife, at the encouragement of the reservation desk, simply called every evening to inquire about cancellations. I must add that the reservation folks were very friendly and more than willing to take her call every night. At approximately two weeks out, as it is common for lots of people to cancel, we ended up getting four nights in one room and two nights at another location in the park—just what we wanted in the first place. If you are persistent, it may very likely pay off. The park accepts reservations for accommodations one year plus one day, 366 days, in advance.

Officially, park lodging consists of the following number of units:

The Ahwahnee	123 units
Yosemite Lodge at the Falls	249 units
Curry Village	499 units
Housekeeping Camp	266 units
Wawona Hotel	104 units
Tuolumne Meadows Lodge	69 units
White Wolf Lodge	28 units
High Sierra Camps (avail. via lottery)	55 units

Finally, there are thirteen campgrounds within the park boundaries of Yosemite. Seven are on a first-come first had basis; the other six require reservations. I'll mark those requiring a reservation with an (RR) for "reservations required." The campgrounds are located at four locations in the valley: North Pines (RR), Upper Pines (RR), Lower Pines (RR), and Camp 4 at Wawona (RR mid-April – late-Sept.), Bridalveil Creek, Tamarack Flat, Crane Flat, Hodgdon Meadow (RR mid-April – early-Oct.), Yosemite Creek, Porcupine Flat, White Wolf, and Tuolumne Meadows (RR, half the sites). There is a fourteenth campground located at Hetch Hetchy. This campground has twenty-five walk-in tent sites, open all year, but restricted to people beginning or ending trips into the back country. A wilderness permit is required. Campground reservations, again for those that operate on a reservation based system, are accepted up to five months in advance.

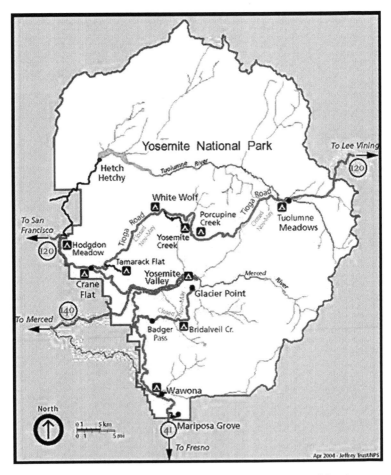

Campground locations at Yosemite National Park

There are also numerous hotel, motel, and cabin accommodations located just outside the park entrances, especially in El Portal, just outside the west entrance, and in the town of Fish Camp, just outside the south entrance. However, most accommodations fill up months in advance, and if you have to or decide to stay somewhere other than in the valley, you are looking at a half hour in and out each day from the west entrance and an hour in and out (along a constantly winding road) if you stay at the south entrance. I'LL STATE IT EMPHATICALLY, RIGHT HERE, THAT THE PARK EXPERIENCE IS BEST IF YOU STAY RIGHT IN THE VALLEY! To wake up and step outside to see Yosemite Falls right in front of you, especially in the crisp late fall air (as I experienced one Thanksgiving week), is worth having to stay in the often worn and well used accommodations of the Yosemite Lodge.

Having said this, I find the town of Fish Camp a very delightful place to stay for a night or two, if you are planning to finish your trip with a day or two at the most southern points of interest, Wawona and the Mariposa Grove, before exiting to the south. There are many nice and relatively small places to stay, as well as the much larger and very nice Tenaya Lodge. Tenaya Lodge is a great place, and basically the only place other than the Ahwahnee Hotel in the valley that is fully equipped for corporate use, if a company wants to combine a meeting with leisure at Yosemite, for example. Fish Camp is only about three miles from the Mariposa Grove, as the town is just outside of the south gate, and the grove is just a mile inside the park's south entrance.

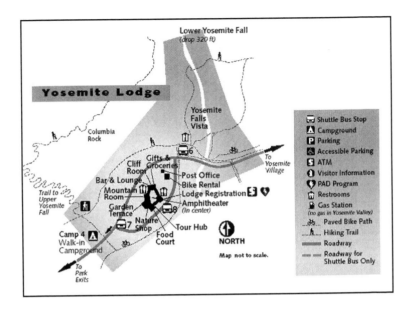

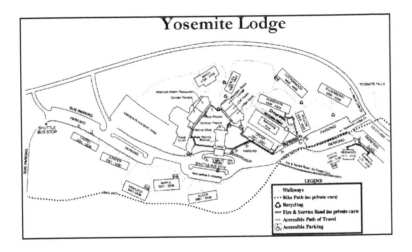

One thing I strongly recommend is requesting information on Yosemite directly from the Park. The address is as follows:

Yosemite National Park
Box 577
Yosemite, California 95389
209-372-0200
www.nps.gov/yose

You will get information on park activities, hiking trails, accommodations within the park, etc. However, they usually give out the addresses of those who request information, and this should result in you getting pamphlets from privately owned hotels and cabins just outside the park.

I have listed the phone numbers and websites in Chapter 9 for the local Chamber of Commerce offices, serving the surrounding towns of Fish Camp, Oakhurst, El Portal, and Lee Vining to assist in your trip planning.

Again, please note that you WILL NOT find the usual chain hotels (thanks goodness). The accommodations just outside the park, for the most part, are very quaint, clean, and possess much more character than the chains you are used to in the more typical vacation hot spots (Orlando for example). Most are great and very nice. They simply are not in as good of a location as accommodations in Yosemite Valley. The only hotel I am aware of that was built by a chain is now no longer part of a chain. This very nice hotel is the Tenaya Lodge in Fish Camp (just outside the south gate). I have stayed here and it is very nice, and it is much cheaper in the off season (non-summer). This was built as a Marriott® but sold off more than a decade ago.

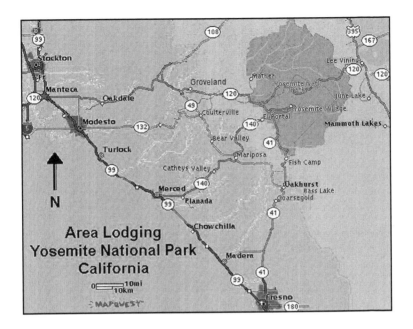

Let's talk some specifics on the Ahwahnee Hotel. I will give a brief history here. A full written history is available for free in the Ahwahnee Lobby. The Ahwahnee came about due to the vision of the first director of the National Park Service, Stephen Mather. Yosemite was his favorite park in the National Park System, and he ordered the park concessionaire (the Yosemite Park and Curry Company) to build a high class hotel to attract wealthy and influential people, in hopes that they would bring their money to Yosemite. Often, this class of traveler will not desire the park experience because they are used to first class hotels, and not rustic cabins or less than pampered service. This is not a criticism; just a necessary explanation to understand the concept behind building the Ahwahnee.

In July of 1925, Gilbert Stanley Underwood was chosen as the architect for the new hotel. Underwood had a

24

Master's degree in Architecture from Harvard and had previously designed lodges at both Zion and Bryce Canyon National Parks. The hotel was built mostly of steel, granite, and concrete, with the exterior stained to look like redwood. This created a hotel very resistant to fire, and today stands as a 150,000 square foot facility, containing ninety-nine rooms, plus twenty-four stand-alone bungalows. The Ahwahnee opened on July 16, 1927, at a cost of $1,250,000, a lot of money for 1927!

During World War II, the Ahwahnee was temporarily turned over to the United States Navy for offices, barracks, and a hospital. Unfortunately, our service personnel took quite a few souvenirs with them when they left, and it took a $400,000 renovation to re-open it to the public in time for Christmas 1946.

The Ahwahnee Hotel

Chapter 6

HIKING OPTIONS

While there are an endless numbers of trails, and far too many to list all of them, allow me to describe some of the best.

Two hikes I have not done are two multiple day endurance hikes. The first is the sixty-mile long High Sierra Loop, which is designed to be navigated in six days, traveling ten miles each day. You'll find an appropriately supplied campsite located at the end of each ten-mile segment to provide a restful and memorable night's stay. The other trail is the John Muir Trail. This highly famous trail follows much of the Sierra Range, with thirty-seven of its 211-mile length stretching through Yosemite. It is easy to experience part of this beautiful and historic trail if you hike to Vernal and Nevada Falls, as you will see later in this chapter.

On the other hand, I have personally done all of the day hikes listed in this chapter, except some of those along the Tioga Road and the Chilnualna Fall hike.

HIKES IN OR NEAR THE YOSEMITE VALLEY
AND ALONG THE GLACIER POINT ROAD

EASY

There are many flat trails, consisting of less than a half-mile each, that lead to spectacular sites.

Hike to the base of Lower Yosemite Fall

This is a flat one-mile round-trip to get you to the base of Lower Yosemite Fall. This is the base of the tallest waterfall in the United States and the fifth highest in the world, Yosemite Falls. You'll get great views of both Upper and Lower Yosemite Fall from here. The falls will be at their best in spring, yet could be dry by fall. It is a must for first time visitors. The hike is very easy and will only take you about twenty minutes, plus whatever time you wish to spend just staring once you get there. The trail is located at Shuttle Bus Stop #6 on the north side of the Yosemite Valley.

Hike to the base of Bridalveil Fall

This is a relatively easy hike that begins and ends on the valley floor and only takes about twenty minutes round-trip. However, be advised that there is a short section of steep incline near the very end. The round trip is only about a half-mile and will get you to the best vantage point for a close up view of a beautiful waterfall. It also allows you to experience the drifting mist from the water. The trail here begins at the Bridalveil Fall Parking Area on the south side of Yosemite Valley.

Walk around the grounds of the Ahwahnee Hotel

Shuttle Bus Stop #3. Self-explanatory.

Hike to Mirror Lake

28

This is a seasonal lake; it often dries up in the fall. It is a flat, easy hike of slightly greater length than those listed above. A two-mile round trip will take you deeper into the far eastern and enclosed end of the Yosemite Valley. This is a good place to possibly see black bears and other wildlife in the valley. It follows a similar path to one you would take if you decide to go horseback riding. The trailhead is located at Shuttle Bus Stop #17.

Walk through the valley on the paved trails and boardwalks and across the bridge over the Merced River

This hike provides 360 degree panoramic views of the walls surrounding the Yosemite Valley.

MODERATE

Trail from Happy Isles to the Vernal Fall footbridge

This offers an unbelievable view of Vernal Fall, and in my opinion, the most beautiful fall in Yosemite. This trail is full of ups and downs but is paved to this point. If you are not physically up to it or simply not interested in doing the entire Mist Trail, I suggest walking this first part of the trail for the view. IT IS WORTH IT! Shuttle Bus Stop #16.

STRENUOUS

The hike to the top of Upper Yosemite Falls

Upper Yosemite Falls drops 1430 feet, the middle cascade drops 675 feet, and the Lower Fall has a 320 foot drop. This is a more than seven-mile round-trip with many switchbacks (a switchback is a zigzag in a road or on a trail that actually increases the length, in order to decrease the degree of incline or decline). The trail is very steep and strenuous and often has one spending many hours in the hot summer sun. Take plenty of water and take it slowly, especially coming down.

This trail can encourage a person to take it a little fast coming down. If you come down too fast and let your legs pound each rock like a shock absorber along the way, you may just end up with a case of elevation change sickness. That is no fun! I have spent many hours with the world spinning and unable to keep food down, if you know what I mean. However, this is also one of the best hikes, and it rewards each hiker with one of the best views in Yosemite. This trail demands a 2,700 foot elevation change and is located near Shuttle Bus Stop #7. Allow at least five to six hours.

The trail to Glacier Point

This is one of my favorite hikes in the park. It comprises a 4.8 mile trail, each way, from the south side of the valley (across from Sentinel Beach and Leidig Meadow, just west of the historic chapel) to the overlook at Glacier Point. The view all the way up just keeps getting better and better.

My wife and I first hiked this trail one Thanksgiving Day, in dense fog. While we risked terrible views all day long from the fog, and the contemplation of better ways to spend the day, we decided that this was our only chance as we were leaving the next day. To our surprise, we climbed just above the fog layer as we neared the top. The view and pictures we got of Half Dome jutting out of the fog, in crystal clear blue skies, were unbelievable. This was one of the most beautiful sights I have ever seen!

This strenuous hike will take you up 3,200 feet from where you start. Allow three to four hours, one way. You have multiple options after reaching Glacier Point. You can climb back down the same trail, take the Panorama Trail and connect to the Mist Trail or the John Muir to return to the valley at Happy Isles (this will add eight more challenging miles and get you back to the valley, a couple of miles from where you started), or you can arrange to have someone pick you up at Glacier Point by car. Shuttle Bus Stop E5.

Half Dome viewed from Glacier Point as both begin to emerge from an early morning fog in November.

The Mist Trail to Vernal and Nevada Falls

This is probably the best trail to take if you just want to take one trail, see unbelievable beauty that you will remember for a lifetime, and hike a difficult trail that the entire family (unless you have small children) can, with some "can-do" mental determination, accomplish. In other words, short of the dangerous hike to the top of Half Dome, this is the best hike in the park. Actually, it is exactly the same hike as the first half of the Half Dome hike.

Having said that, there is a price to pay. This is also usually the most populated trail in the park. This trail is best in the off season, anytime other than summer. August is the month of peak visitation for Yosemite. However, I took this trail on July 26, 2008, and despite the crowds, it was still very much worth it.

The trail starts with approximately a mile of paved walkway and a gradual incline. The paved portion ends at the foot bridge, where you can get a great view of Vernal Fall. Vernal Fall (317 foot drop) is, in my opinion, the most beautiful thing to see in the park. If you are not up to this entire hike, at least come this far for the view.

From this point on, the trail gets strenuous at various points, such as the final approach to Nevada Fall (594-foot drop). The mist from the falling water hitting the rocks below Vernal Fall provides one of the best photo opportunities in the entire park. This spot is where the Mist Trail gets its name. There are rock stairs laid out and maintained by the excellent national park service teams. They are responsible for the 800-plus miles of trails throughout the park with funds provided through the Yosemite Fund. The stairs to get you up, over, and to the continuing trail above Vernal Fall are safely constructed with hand railings. Believe me, it is breathtaking beauty, safe, and a real "must see."

From this point, the trail gets easier, flatter, and takes you along Emerald Pool. There is NO SWIMMING. Remember, you never want to swim in water above falls, no matter how calm and safe it may seem. It isn't safe. As you approach Nevada Fall, you once again have to negotiate steep and strenuous stairs to get to the top of the falls. This ends the Mist Trail and gets you to a very rewarding spot to consume the lunch in your backpack. This hike, with an hour of rest at the top and then a return to the valley via the same trial or the John Muir Trail, can fill most of an entire day. However, if you want to prove how unbelievably capable you are as a hiker, you can continue on to the top of Half Dome or take the Panorama Trail to Glacier Point. More on both of these trails under their listings. Shuttle Bus Stop #16.

Vernal Fall

Nevada Fall

The Panorama Trail

This is a moderate to strenuous hike. It is often listed as moderate because there is no single highly strenuous part. However, the length of this hike, about four miles one way, and the many up and down portions while navigating through switchbacks makes it more than your typically moderate hike. This trail offers stunning views of the valley below, thick forests, and the only way to see Illilouette Fall (370 foot drop, don't step too close to the edge). It is beautiful and offers lots of sunshine and solitude.

This trail starts out just to the right (or south) from Glacier Point and is not too heavily used. At the half-way point it crosses (via a well-constructed foot bridge) Illilouette Creek that leads to Illilouette Fall and offers a stunning spot to stop for lunch and just enjoy the pine forest and the sound of rushing water. This spot is, in my opinion, one of the most beautiful places in the entire park.

I want to be clear here! While the Panorama Trail is a connector trail and is technically by itself about four miles in length one-way as stated above; you must plan for an 8.0 to 8.5 mile day of hiking as you must either turn-around and return to Glacier Point, or connect to and use the Mist Trail or the John Muir Trail to get to the valley floor below, arriving at Happy Isles. Plan on a much longer and much more strenuous day if you connect to the trail to the top of Half Dome. It took me five visits to Yosemite to explore the Panorama Trail; I wish I'd explored it sooner.

Along the Panorama Trail

The granddaddy of them all: the Half Dome Hike!

Ok, if you are reading this page and considering the Half Dome hike, you are considering one of the most memorable days of your life. If you're a rock climber who has climbed the granite face of El Capitan, a sky diver, or a bungee jumper, you will not find this to be all that challenging or rewarding. However, if you are a mere mortal like me, just a day hiker who loves the parks, and want to experience the ultimate in day hiking, this is the one. Let me also state that this hike is not for the careless or those who are deathly afraid of heights. In my experiences, the only national park hikes that rank with the Half Dome hike are Angel's Landing at Zion and the hikes down the north and south rims of the Grand Canyon.

This hike is basically an extension of the Mist Trail hike. It extends the eight-mile round-trip of the Mist Trail to an all day, seventeen-mile endurance hike. Be sure to get an early start. The trail above Nevada Falls is actually fairly easy to moderate for the first three miles through Little Yosemite Valley. Then it gets quite steep, with switchbacks cut into rock and tight paths to share with those coming down the trail.

The difficulty in this hike is two-fold: the length of the trail and the ascent at the trail's end up the side of Half Dome. The final 400+ feet are at a 60 degree climb up the east side of Half Dome, allowing you to stand on the very top. The park service has constructed cables that they leave up seasonally, spring through mid fall. The cables would probably hold a military tank in suspension, but are flexible and move freely as you hold on for dear life. The cables are threaded through posts that are planted in drilled holes in the granite. However, these move freely up and down and offer a simple two-by-four to rest on, about every fifteen feet.

The risk here is slipping and not having a death grip on the cable, being up there (foolishly) when lightening is possible, having someone above you on the cables fall and take you out with them, or getting to the top and freezing up at the thought of coming down.

In fact, Yosemite National Park, acknowledging the danger involved in overcrowding on the final cables portion of this hike, is implementing an interim program beginning in 2010 requiring a day-use permit on Fridays, Saturdays, Sundays, and all federal holidays. 400 Permits will be issued for each day costing $1.50 each and must be obtained in advance. The permits are required only for the top section of the hike from the base of the sub-dome to the summit of Half Dome which includes the cables section. As a point of reference, in 2008, about 84,000 people climbed to the top of Half Dome, estimated at just fewer than 400 per day on weekdays, yet as high as 1,200 on peak days. 100 (of the 400) permits will be reserved for those with the appropriate wilderness permits at no additional charge. You can request up to four permits per request at www.recreation.gov (preferred) or by calling 877-444-6777 (877-833-6777 TDD or 518-885-3639 from outside the US & Canada); permits will be sent via e-mail or regular mail. Permits for May and June are available beginning March 1, July and August permits available beginning April 1, and September and October permits are available beginning May 1. The cables are normally up from around the third Friday in May through Columbus Day Monday. The cables are not guaranteed to be in place on any given day and are very "iffy" in May and October.

Also, PLEASE, leave your backpack at the bottom of the cable portion, but zip it closed so the squirrels don't eat your food. You can do without it for the hour you will be on the dome. I cannot tell you how many people going the opposite way hit me with their overloaded backpacks; it's scary!

Also, be sure to pick up, use, and return a pair of gloves from the pile provided at the base of the cable portion. (I am starting the rumor, right here, that it is bad luck to get a mismatched pair).

Having said all the required warnings so that you take this hike seriously, it is well worth it and a must if you are up to the challenge and can afford to dedicate an entire day to this experience. Be sure to take a camera (I suggest disposable) with you on this hike. You will want the memories. You will especially want to get a good photo of yourself standing on the top so that the next day you can go to the valley general store and purchase the picture frame that says, "I made it to the top!"

Lastly, don't take your pre-teen kids on this hike, and not even the teenagers unless they are physically and mentally very mature. It's not about showing them everything you get to see. It's about ensuring that you do not witness them fall to their death right in front of you on your vacation! You need to know that recent fatal accidental falls from the final cables section of this hike include two in 2007 and one in 2009. There was one serious injury, near-fatal accident exactly one week prior to the 2009 fatal accident as well. I suggest google-ing "Half Dome Cables" as you plan your trip. There is a lot out there to assist you in envisioning what you might be getting into on this hike. Shuttle Bus Stop #16.

Nearing the end and most difficult part of the Half Dome Hike, as you approach from the seldom seen east side. Cables can be seen in the distance.

39

Half Dome Cables

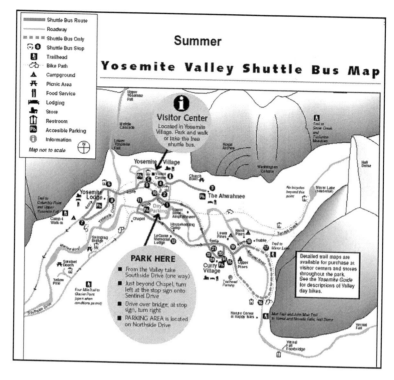

HIKES ALONG THE TIOGA ROAD,
INCLUDING TUOLUMNE MEADOWS

These trails are in the higher elevations, where relatively fewer people go.

Lembert Dome

The hike up Lembert Dome is probably the most known and traveled trail in this part of the park. This is a relatively moderate two- to three-hour hike to the top of the granite dome and includes a great view overlooking Tuolumne Meadows. The hike is nearly three miles and includes a modest elevation gain of 900 feet. The trailhead is located on the Tioga Road at the far eastern edge of

Tuolumne Meadows, in the parking area at road marker T-32, east of the bridge over the Tuolumne River. It is forty miles east of Crane Flat and seven miles west of the Tioga Pass entrance.

Other hikes from the Tuolumne Meadows area include numerous hikes to beautiful high country lakes including:

Cathedral Lake

This is a four- to six-hour round trip and a moderately strenuous hike that will take you approximately eight miles, with views of numerous glacial peaks and domes along the way. Lower Cathedral Lake is beneath Cathedral Lake, and the Upper Cathedral Lake is just below Cathedral Pass. You will experience a 1000-foot elevation change. The trailhead is located at the west end of Tuolumne Meadows, west of Budd Creek, at the parking lot on the south side of Tioga Road. It is thirty-eight miles east of Crane Flat and nine miles west of the Tioga Pass entrance.

Elizabeth Lake

This hike is about a five-mile round-trip, moderately strenuous, and will take you about four hours. You'll experience a 900-foot elevation gain en route to see one of the most beautiful alpine lakes anywhere. Elizabeth Lake was carved by a glacier and is located at the base of Unicorn Peak. If you can handle chilly water, Elizabeth Lake is a great place for a safe swim. You'll get great up-close views of both Unicorn and Johnson Peaks. The trailhead is located along the Tioga Road thirty-nine miles east of Crane Flat and eight miles west of the Tioga Pass entrance. It is at the far end of the Tuolumne Meadows Campground, near Group Camp.

Glen Aulin

This is a more strenuous trail. You will need to allow eight to ten hours. It follows the Tuolumne River through small Aspen forests. Sights on this trail include the Glen Aulin camping area, Tuolumne Falls, and the White Cascade.

This is what I call a reverse hike. In other words, know your capabilities because it is downhill, at first, and then uphill to return. Downhill is always easier and can cause people to overextend themselves and have problems making the return trip on the trail. This regularly causes a very serious situation at the Grand Canyon. This is nothing close to the extremes there! This is a lengthy fourteen-mile round trip. It requires an 800-foot elevation gain on the return, and can be found at Soda Springs. The parking lot is just north of Tioga Road, at road marker T-32. It is east of the bridge over the Tuolumne River, thirty-eight miles east of Crane Flat.

HIKES ALONG THE TIOGA ROAD, BUT NOT AT TUOLUMNE MEADOWS

These hikes mostly include beautiful, small lakes:

May Lake

An easy 1.25-mile, three-hour hike to a high Sierra camp. The round-trip in 2.5 miles, involves only a 400-foot elevation change and can be located at the May Lake parking area, north of the Tioga Road, at road marker T-21. The trailhead is twenty-eight miles east of Crane Flat and twenty miles west of the Tioga Pass entrance. Drive, from this point, two miles to the parking lot.

Sunrise Lakes

Here is a more strenuous hike up the side of the Tenaya Canyon. Get ready for beautiful views of Clouds Rest and Tenaya Lake. Here are three Sunrise Lakes, the first on the right and the latter two on your left. All offer good swimming locations. The entire hike is five to seven hours and is approximately 7.5 miles. Find the trailhead on the Tioga Road thirty-one miles east of Crane Flat at the southwest end of Tenaya Lake.

Gaylor and Granite Lakes

This is a fantastic high Sierra hike. The hike is a six-mile round-trip and should take about four to five hours. The elevation gain is nearly 1,000 feet and will take you to three Gaylor Lakes, two Granite Lakes, plus an old Sierra ghost mine. The trailhead can be found just inside the Tioga Pass Entrance, forty-eight miles east of Crane Flat on the north side of Tioga Road.

Mono Pass

This is a very old and historic trail. It was used by miners and explorers. You'll see old mining cabins and the old Golden Crown Mine remnants. Look to see great views of Mt. Gibbs and Mono Lake. The hike is eight miles round-trip and can be located on the south side of Tioga Road at road marker T-37, 5.5 miles east of Tuolumne Meadows. It is 1.5 miles west of the Tioga Pass entrance and forty-six miles east of Crane Flat.

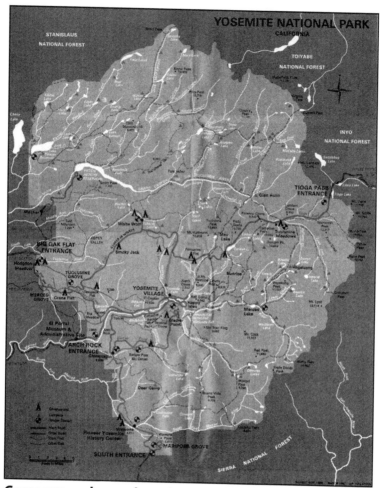

Campground map, but also one of the best at showing points along the Tioga Road

WAWONA and THE MARIPOSA GROVE HIKES

Wawona to Chilnualna Falls

This six- to eight-hour round-trip excursion provides up close views of rock formations and a view of the secluded Chilnualna Falls. It is a cascading type waterfall, not the high free falling type like you see in the valley. Still, it is quite beautiful in its own way. It is similar to Wapama Fall at Hetch Hetchy. The entire hike is just over eight miles and includes a respectable 2,500 foot elevation gain. The trailhead is located at the parking lot, nearly two miles out Chilnualna Falls Road from Highway 41, just prior to the paved road turning to dirt.

Upper and Lower Grove hikes at the Mariposa Grove

There are numerous ways to navigate through the Mariposa Grove. One-way distances range from .8 miles to see the Grizzly Giant, just over two miles to the Grove Museum, to a full three miles to the Wawona Point overlook. You can judge your own distance here based upon how you are feeling. There are many named trees (many of the larger trees have been given names like the Galen Clark Tree, after the man believed to have discovered the grove, or the Clothespin Tree because it looks like a giant clothespin), all with their own interesting story, yet looking very much alike. You can also purchase a seat on the tram if your legs are getting tired from many days of walking around this magnificent park.

The Grizzly Giant, lower Mariposa Grove

I strongly suggest hiking to the Wawona Point Overlook. It is one additional, basically-flat mile beyond the Fallen Wawona Tunnel Tree. This is another fantastic place to take your lunch break. You can see for many miles and can see the main highway far below, as well as the clearing of the nine-hole golf course at Wawona. On pristine days, they claim you can see the very distant California Coastal Range. Again, the view is spectacular, and you usually have this spot to yourself.

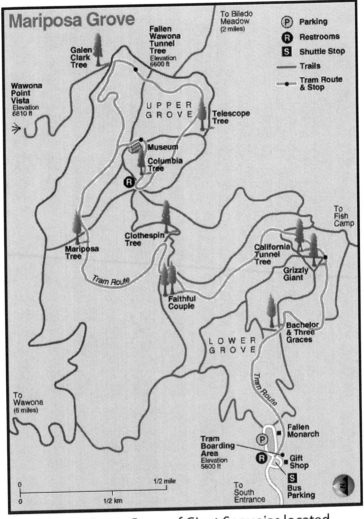

The Mariposa Grove of Giant Sequoias located near the south entrance to Yosemite National Park

48

OTHER PARK HIKING TRAIL LOCATIONS

Hike down to the Tuolumne Grove of Giant Sequoias

The Tuolumne Grove contains approximately twenty-five trees and is located near Crane Flat, at the intersection of Big Oak Flat and Tioga Roads. This path is only accessible on foot (open to automobiles many years ago) and drops about 500 feet. This hike is relatively short, yet also relatively strenuous on the way back up!

Hike down to the Merced Grove of Giant Sequoias

The Merced Grove contains approximately twenty trees and is also only accessible on foot. This four-mile hike will take you about three hours round-trip. The trailhead is located 3.5 miles north of Crane Flat and 4.5 miles south of the Big Oak Flat Entrance, on Highway 120 west, marked by road sign B-10.

Tunnel to Wapama Falls at Hetch Hetchy Reservoir

Taking the drive out Highway 120, exiting the park boundary, and then returning in through Camp Mather to see Hetch Hetchy is a really fantastic thing to do and a way to brag about seeing a part of this beautiful park that even many multiple-time visitors will have to admit they have never experienced. Once you arrive at the Hetch Hetchy Reservoir, take the walk across the dam and through the tunnel to get to the trailhead. There are multiple destinations, but the most common is going as far as Wapama Falls. This is an easy to moderate hike, covering about five miles and taking at least three hours. The reservoir is beautiful. You can use your imagination to visualize how this valley would rival the Yosemite Valley if it weren't damned up. There is no swimming allowed in the reservoir.

Wapama Falls, as viewed across Hetch Hetchy Reservoir

Chapter 7

I DON'T WANT OR LIKE TO HIKE, WHAT ELSE CAN I DO?

Yosemite offers more recreation options than I could possibly list. However, options range from ice skating at the Curry Village Ice Rink, snowshoeing, sledding, cross-country skiing, backcountry ski tours, downhill skiing and snowboarding (at Badger Pass) in winter, mule and horseback riding, rental bike riding on many miles of paved trails, rock climbing, rock climbing lessons, hiking, group hiking, fishing, bird watching, golf, photography, or wading and swimming (be careful, and NEVER enter water upstream from a waterfall) in summer. Shopping is even an option, including mostly souvenir items, from t-shirts to mugs and fine art. One of the finest outdoor specialty shops in the country is located at Yosemite, the Mountain Shop at Curry Village.

Wading in the Merced River in the valley or under the covered bridge at the Pioneer Yosemite History Center are relatively safe places to do this. Swimming is also allowed in most of the alpine lakes, reached via trails along the Tioga Road. Some of these are fairly cold; the shallower ones are the warmest. Remember that you can NEVER SWIM UPSTREAM OF A WATERFALL! It is a great way to lose your life!

Speaking of waterfalls, the following are the main waterfalls in Yosemite, with their height and location:

Yosemite Falls (2,425 feet)	valley wall – north side
Chilnualna Falls (2,200 feet)	hiking trail from Wawona
Sentinel Falls (1,920 feet)	valley wall – south side
Ribbon Fall (1,612 feet)	valley wall – north side
Wapama Falls (1,400 feet)	Hetch Hetchy – north side
Horsetail Fall (1,000 feet)	east side wall of El Capitan
Bridalveil Fall (620 feet)	valley wall – south side
Nevada Fall (594 feet)	along the Mist Trail
Illilouette Fall (370 feet)	along the Panorama Trail
Vernal Fall (317 feet)	along the Mist Trail

You can't rank the waterfalls in order of beauty by simply using relative height. First of all, they are all extremely beautiful. Having said that, some are free-falling while others bounce off cascades or a non-vertical wall that juts out. For example, I believe that Vernal is clearly the most beautiful (note it is actually the shortest on the list). However, the width and amount of water that plunges over a sheer cliff, falling straight down in a rainbow mist, bracketed by lush green growth, to first crash on rock below and then calm down and transform into the Merced River makes it an unbelievable sight. Also, the rock formations along the Mist Trail, plus the effort you must give to get to the best viewing points along this trail, make it even more beautiful and rewarding. Vernal Fall and Nevada Fall are both visible and quite beautiful from Glacier Point, but if you really want to say you saw these great falls, take the

Mist Trail, along with scores of other visitors, on one of the park's most traveled hikes, to see them up close..

Also, while Yosemite Falls, Chilnualna Falls, and Sentinel Falls are the three tallest, none of them are free-falling. Chilnualna is a cascading type, made up of numerous small sections, while Yosemite is divided into three sections: the upper, middle, and lower falls, and Sentinel is in six main sections.

Illilouette and Chilnualna Falls are only visible via hiking; neither can be seen from a road. Illilouette can be reached by taking the Panorama Trail from Glacier Point or the Mist Trail from the valley and hooking into the Panorama Trail at the top of Nevada Fall. Chilnualna Falls can be reached via a rather steep trail from Wawona.

Lastly, Ribbon, Horsetail, and Sentinel Falls are all seasonal, drying up in April, late May, and July, respectively. All others listed here flow year-round, with peak flow occurring in May, due to seasonal snow melting at higher elevations.

~

Horses and mules are available at three stable locations: Tuolumne (in the high country), the Yosemite Valley, and Wawona. You must arrive at least one hour prior to your ride and meet the minimum requirements: seven years of age, forty-four inches tall, and a weight of no more than 225 pounds.

~

In the heart of the Yosemite Valley, you will find many museums, historical sites, and buildings. There are shops, an Ansel Adams Art Gallery, the Yosemite Museum, the Yosemite Cemetery, live Yosemite Theatre, the LeConte

Memorial Lodge, the Ahwahnee Hotel, the Valley Wilderness Center, and more at and surrounding the Yosemite Valley Visitor Center. At the far east end of the valley is the Happy Isles Nature Center.

Yosemite Valley Visitor Center

This location has a very nice exhibit hall where the origins of the Yosemite landscape are displayed. There are exhibits on various people who have lived in Yosemite through the centuries, on wildlife and vegetation in the park, as well as an excellent short film on the park and all it has to offer visitors.

Yosemite Museum

The museum is next to the visitor center and displays exhibits on Native Americans, natural history, and wildlife exhibits. You can learn how basket-weaving and jewelry making were done. There is a very well-done reconstruction of the village of the Ahwahnee natives behind the museum.

You will not want to miss the new section of the Yosemite Museum titled, "Granite Frontiers: A Century of Yosemite Climbing". It opened in 2008 and pays a historic, factual, and pictorial tribute to the years of granite rock climbing on El Capitan. This unbelievable climb takes most climbers three or more days. The record climb currently stands at a mind-blowing 2 hours, 37 minutes, 5 seconds!

Yosemite Cemetery

The cemetery is just west of the Museum, on the other side of the street. Here lies the final resting place for Native Americans and certain individuals who played a critical role in the history and development of Yosemite National Park.

The Ansel Adams Gallery

This gallery displays and sells (you guessed it) the great work of Ansel Adams, as well as the works of other photographers and artists. This is also an excellent place to get books, photography supplies, and souvenirs.

The Ahwahnee Hotel

This hotel is more fully described in Chapter 5 and is a National Historic Landmark. It is a "must see," regardless of whether or not one is staying there, due to its sheer beauty, rustic décor, and historical significance.

The LeConte Memorial Lodge

This lodge was Yosemite's first visitor center and is also designated a National Historic Landmark. It is open May through September and features a library, as well as children's, environmental, and various evening programs.

Happy Isles Nature Center

The nature center features natural history and wildlife exhibits. Nearby are short trails to educate visitors on the area's four different environments: forest, river, talus (rock debris at the base of a cliff), and fen (low land partially or fully covered with water). It is located just a short walk south from the Happy Isles Shuttle Bus Stop (Shuttle Bus Stop #16) and is operated May through September.

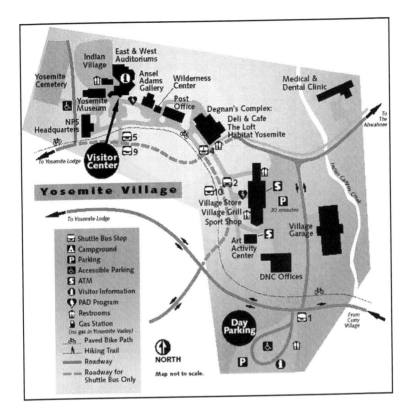

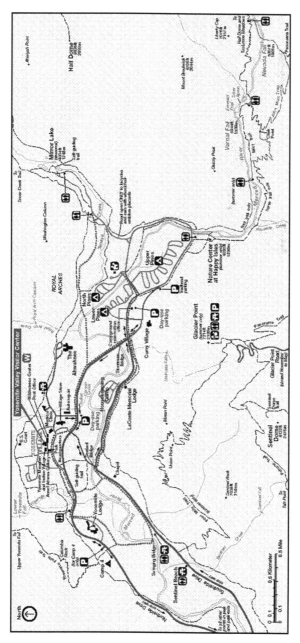

Map of Yosemite Valley destinations

I better make a few comments about rock climbing: I am not a climber and never will be. I would probably sooner bungee-jump. I am not trying to put down climbing, quite the opposite. I am just being honest enough to admit that I am too "chicken" to even consider it. I get nervous just climbing the ladder to wash the upstairs windows on my house. However, granite wall rock climbing is a really big thing at Yosemite. El Capitan is the premier spot to climb in the country, and I have stood in awe watching climbers each and every time I have visited. If you visit the Yosemite Valley, you will most probably watch climbers, if you are not one of the small percentage who actually participates (note the comments under the Yosemite Museum concerning the exhibit on climbing El Capitan). This hike normally takes three or more days.

Yes, Yosemite is known as one of the world's greatest climbing spots. There are numerous places to climb besides El Capitan. There are day climbs on the various domes of the Tuolumne Meadows area and multi day-climbs on the walls of the valley. While deaths do occur, the percentage is thankfully quite low. However, the number of individuals who climb the 90 degree walls of the valley number in the thousands each year, and over one hundred climbing accidents occur annually.

Of the hundred or more accidents, approximately 25 percent require rescue. You should practice self-rescue techniques and know what to do in a serious emergency. Know your route. Study your route extensively prior to any climbing event, and realize that being rescued is not guaranteed. In other words, Yosemite is not the place for beginning rock climbing or attempting to learn by "trial and error."

Remember that rescues seriously endanger the lives of rescue personnel and those necessitating the rescue. They also cost a lot of money. If you necessitate rescue by helicopter, it is critically important that you do EXACTLY what the rescue personnel instruct you to do. The Yosemite Medical Clinic is set up and prepared to handle the unfortunate climbing injury.

Also, be sure to check with park rangers, the Camp 4 kiosk, or the Mountain Shop for climbing routes currently restricted due to Peregrine Falcon nesting sites.

Finally, Wilderness Permits are not required for nights spent sleeping/hanging from the canyon walls. However, there are rules with which you need to comply:

1) Do not litter, and if you take it up, bring it down.
2) Do not build windbreaks, platforms, or other improvements.
3) Do not create new fire rings. If you must have a fire, use a fire ring that already exists.
4) Do not throw anything from the walls.
5) Do not leave fixed ropes as permanent attachments on approach or descent routes.
6) Do not pass other parties without gaining their permission.
7) Do not leave anything (food or beverage) at the top or along the way for other parties.
8) Finally, you must carry a plastic container or bag, or what I have heard referred to as a "poop tube." I believe the purpose here is self-explanatory! After you descend from your climb, dump human waste in a pit toilet. You can dump paper in a pit toilet, but never plastic.

∾

For evening entertainment, remember that you will not get much in the way of radio reception in the park.

The only exception is the park information radio station. Actually, you can get television, but only select stations via satellite at the Ahwahnee and the Yosemite Lodge at the Falls. However, do you really want to travel to a national park to watch television?

My family and I always take in as many evening ranger talks as possible. They are offered at various places in the park, including the Yosemite Lodge Amphitheater, the Curry Village Amphitheater, and the Lower Pines Campground Amphitheater, all located in the Yosemite Valley, plus the Wawona Campground Amphitheater located in the southern part of the park. These are free interactive lectures, talks, or slide shows, lasting about an hour (usually beginning at 8:30 pm but check to be sure). They are incredibly informing, relaxing, and the perfect way to wind down the day. Daily topics are often on a seven-day rotation and may include presentations on wildlife, fires in the park, changing seasons, the first park settlers, early mining in the park, etc.

~

For the winter visitor who prefers winter sports, Yosemite features the often overlooked Badger Pass Ski Resort and Lodge. Badger Pass is at an elevation of 7,200 feet and is located midway between the valley and Wawona, just a quick five-mile drive up Glacier Point Road. While Glacier Point Road is officially listed as closed in winter, it is open nearly year-round as far as Badger Pass.

The Badger Pass Ski Lodge was originally constructed in 1935 (the same year the Glacier Point Road opened) and was the first alpine ski lodge in the state of California. It has undergone numerous modifications and repairs through the years and is today in great need of repair and upgrades to meet current codes and provide adequate services for visitors. Yosemite National Park is currently assessing a major rehabilitation project for the facility.

Badger Pass features ninety acres of skiing with ten runs and five lifts. The base is at 7,200 feet, the summit at 8,000 feet. When Los Angeles was selected for the 1932 Summer Olympics, there was some promotion of this area for the Winter Games. However, Lake Placid, New York was eventually selected.

Badger Pass not only offers downhill skiing and snowboarding, but it also provides twenty-two miles of groomed cross-country track and ninety miles of marked trails. There are guided cross-country ski trips offered, including a twenty-one-mile loop from Badger Pass to Glacier Point. The views of Half Dome from Glacier Point, in winter, are said to be unbelievable. Ski equipment is available for rental, by the day, at the lodge.

～

However, if you really want to see Yosemite and do it right, remember to take the following advice. GET BEYOND THE VALLEY! Probably the best activity of all is simply getting in your car and driving through this massive and beautiful park—all 1,169 square miles of it. If you plan the time and get to Wawona and the Mariposa Grove, Hetch Hetchy or Glacier Point, or spend quality time along Tioga Road, you can truly say you have seen Yosemite.

By the way, be sure you have plenty of gas. There is NO GAS available to the public IN THE VALLEY. You can tank up just outside the west or south entrances or within the park, year-round, at Wawona (south) and Crane Flat (west), and seasonally just up the road from the Tuolumne Meadows Visitors Center (northeast) on Tioga Road by the Tuolumne Meadows Mountaineering School/Shop. Believe it or not, my experience has been that gas in Yosemite is cheaper than gas purchased just outside the park!

A drive through Yosemite can easily fill an entire day. Presuming you are starting from lodging in the valley, let me list five options for an unbelievable day.

Option One

Take a drive north and east along Tioga Road. This will take you through higher country with less vegetation and more lakes. This route also gets you far away from the sometimes quite crowded valley. There are no world record waterfalls or Giant Sequoias along this route, simply unbelievable blue skies, alpine lakes, and numerous hiking options.

Activities at and near Tuolumne Meadows on Tioga Road include swimming in the Tuolumne River or any one of the numerous, beautiful alpine lakes. You can rent horses and go riding at the Tuolumne Meadow Stable. There are a wealth of rock climbing and hiking options, and if you are lucky, there are bighorn sheep to watch.

You can go fishing in rivers and streams, from late April through November 15th, or year round in any lake. All fishermen sixteen years of age or older need a California state fishing license. The use of live bait is prohibited.

I highly suggest starting your day with an early visit to the Tuolumne Meadows Visitor Center. Park rangers and visitor center displays will greatly assist the planning of your day. You should also consider purchasing a book on Tioga Road hiking trails, especially if hiking becomes your plan for the day.

Also, as you stop along this route, you are quite likely to see yellow-bellied marmots, large beaver-looking animals, which are not usually seen in the valley. They live at tree line and are most easily seen at Olmsted Point. They are the largest members of the squirrel family and are harmless. However, keep food close as they are beggars and very bold! They may very likely die if they do get to your food; human food is an unnatural diet for all park animals.

This route, if taken all the way to the northeast entrance, will take you through high country and some of the more mountainous and toughest to build roads in the park. You can exit the park at the northeast entrance, Tioga Pass, to visit areas out side the park, such as Mono Lake, Mono Craters, or the town of Lee Vining. You might also want to turn around and make your way back to the valley for dinner.

Option Two

Take highway 120 west and then northwest to Camp Mather. Then take the Hetch Hetchy Road, located just beyond the Big Oak Flat Entrance Station, northeast to Hetch Hetchy. Hetch Hetchy is one of the least visited yet most beautiful parts of Yosemite National Park. It took three visits for me to learn about Hetch Hetchy. It took my fifth visit until the road was open, without bridge construction or major road work, to actually visit this remote area of the park.

The O'Shaughnessy Dam was built, among great protest, in 1923, then raised to its current height in 1938 to create the main water supply for the city of San Francisco, over two hundred miles to the west. This controversial dam filled up a valley that in many ways rivals the Yosemite Valley. Here you can park, walk through a lengthy tunnel cut into a mountain, and get to trails that basically follow the banks of the reservoir and lead to additional Yosemite waterfalls. This is a fantastic area to see, and one that will lead many who have been to Yosemite to ask you where on earth your pictures were taken.

Hetch Hetchy Reservoir

Option Three

Take Highway 120, also called the Big Oak Flat Road, just a short distance to the northwest from the Yosemite Valley to visit one or both of the two Giant Sequoia groves near the Valley (Merced and Tuolumne). These can be skipped if time is limited and you are planning to visit the much larger Mariposa Grove, located near the south entrance. However, if you are not visiting the southern part of the park and are entering and exiting from the west, northwest, or northeast entrances, then both the Merced and Tuolumne groves provide opportunities to see equally impressive Giant Sequoia trees, simply a much smaller number of specimens.

The Merced Grove is the smallest and least visited grove of Giant Sequoias in Yosemite. There exist about twenty trees, accessible only by foot. A four-mile round-trip hiking trail is located 3.5 miles north of Crane Flat, on Highway 120 west or 4.5 miles south of the Big Oak Flat entrance.

The Tuolumne Grove is comprised of about twenty-five trees, near the intersection of the Big Oak Flat and Tioga Roads. This road, now a path and closed to cars, drops 500 feet in about a mile. The trail is moderately steep when returning uphill to the parking area.

Option Four

Take the nearly one-hour drive from the valley to spend a day at the Mariposa Grove of Giant Sequoias (thirty-five miles south of the Yosemite Valley), the Wawona Hotel and golf area, and the Pioneer Yosemite History Center. The southern part of Yosemite is very different from the valley. It provides the massive upper and lower groves of Giant Sequoia trees at Mariposa; an old-time, relaxing experience at the Wawona Hotel; and historical buildings and artifacts from the yesteryears of Yosemite at the Pioneer Yosemite History Center. Allow me to elaborate on these three attractions.

The Mariposa Grove is one of three Giant Sequoia Groves in Yosemite. There are many in southern and central California, yet they remain only a fraction of the Sequoia trees existing thousands of years ago. In other words, see them while you can. Our great, great grandchildren may learn about them only through books, similar to the way we all learn about dinosaurs. The Giant Sequoia is not quite as tall as a Coastal Redwood, but due to their circumference, they are by volume the largest living things on earth.

While Mariposa is one of three groves in Yosemite, it is BY FAR the largest. The Merced Grove has about twenty trees, Tuolumne has about twenty-five, and Mariposa has about five hundred! It is well worth the trip to the southern part of the park to see these giants. A few are visible from the Mariposa Grove parking lot, and larger specimens are just a short distance down the trails. Many trees there are approximately 290 feet tall and over 30 feet in diameter. Some are over three thousand years old. Think about any event in history within the past three thousand years and realize that while it was happening (for instance, Columbus discovering America), the tree you are standing next to was standing in the same spot then. In this forest, time stands still.

There are many named trees here, each with its own significance. I won't list them all here. There is a brochure available at the trailhead. However, I will mention one: the Grizzly Giant. This is believed to be the fifth largest tree in the world. The two largest are located just a few hours south at Kings Canyon and Sequoia National Parks (see Chapter 14), and that makes it the largest in Yosemite. It is estimated to be over 2,700 years old and has a mind-boggling statistic. The large branch that juts out horizontally, directly above your head as you stand under the tree is believed to be bigger in circumference than any tree trunk east of the Mississippi River!

There are plenty of trails here, an optional tram tour, a fallen tunnel tree (they do not cut tunnels anymore), the Grove Museum, bathrooms, and a small souvenir shop where you can get t-shirts and ice cream novelties. One important tip: COME EARLY! The parking lot in mid-summer usually fills up within the first hour. You will then be forced to park at another location, like Wawona, and take a shuttle. This is a popular destination, with limited parking strictly enforced.

While seeing a Giant Sequoia is something everyone should do in their lifetime, I come to Yosemite as much for the sight and smell of the Ponderosa Pine Tree as anything. Its smell reminds me of vanilla. The bark has a reddish tint with deep black crevasses patterned similar to that of the neck of a Giraffe. I better stop here or I will have to write another chapter (heck, one could write an entire book) on the trees and vegetation of Yosemite.

The Pioneer Yosemite History Center takes you back in time. Collected on this site are buildings and vehicles from the early years of Yosemite. You can stroll through a blacksmith shop, get inside a prison cell, or stroll past old, horse-drawn carriages or across a beautiful covered bridge, to name just a few. The center is always open, well marked, and has brochures available.

The Wawona Hotel, while not as high class and expensive as the Ahwahnee, is still a very beautiful place and designated a National Historic Landmark. It is of Victorian California architecture and has one hundred four rooms, fifty with private baths and fifty-four without. The hotel dates from the 1850s and is open mid-March through early January, possibly select winter weekends as well. Amenities include a dining room, swimming pool, nine-hole golf course, and a tennis court. Be sure to visit the Thomas Hill Studio on the grounds of the Wawona Hotel. It features his fine paintings, as well as a good selection of books for sale.

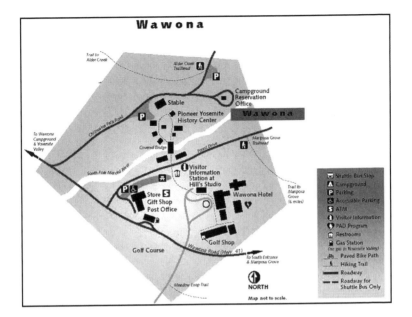

<u>Option Five</u>

Take the road to Glacier Point. This overlook allows a panoramic view, down 3,214 feet to the valley floor. From Glacier Point, you can look east for a fantastic view of Half Dome, or look down to see both Vernal and Nevada Falls. You can look to the valley floor to the north and see the Merced River winding through the valley, plus the Yosemite Lodge area, Yosemite Village, and the beautiful and famous Ahwahnee Hotel.

From here you can hike down to the valley, via the Glacier Point trail, or hike the Panorama Trail to see Illilouette Fall (the only way to see this beautiful and secluded fall) and then connect into the Mist Trail or the John Muir Trail to get to both Vernal and Nevada Falls. This trail ends at Happy Isles, where the valley bus system will give you a free ride to nearly any place on the valley floor.

One constructive comment for the National Park Service: There is no reasonable fee for a bus to take hikers from the valley floor to Glacier Point. A nominal charge, no frills, "no narration, just get me there" type of hiker's bus is needed. There is only a costly one-way trip where the hiker tags along with those taking the Glacier Point Bus Tour. In the winter, there is a free bus from the valley to Badger Pass for skiers, plus a reasonable charge summer hiker's bus to the high country and Tuolumne Meadows area, why not a separate and nominal fee for a hiker's bus, in summer, to Glacier Point?

My son and I were able to hike the Panorama and Mist Trails only because my wife was willing to not participate. She drove us up to Glacier Point and dropped us off. Again, the only other way is to take the one-way fare on the Glacier Point Tour Bus. That is, if you are willing to pay $25 and if you want to feel out of place as a hiker in a rush to get to your trailhead, amongst a group of people who want, deserve, and paid for a slow and narrated relaxing day trip to Glacier Point.

There is the option of hiking up from the valley on the Glacier Point Trail; however, this adds four miles and another strenuous hike to the already planned, eight-mile, strenuous Panorama and Mist Trail hikes. I fail to understand that they can offer a totally free bus system to get around the valley floor and another to get skiers in winter from the valley up to Badger Pass, yet do not offer a reasonable and specifically designated hikers bus to Glacier Point during summer. I have an old brochure from 1990 that proves they once did. Alright, enough, I made my point.

Back to the subject of our day trip. The road up to Glacier Point offers many places to stop and get a terrific view from the top of the valley wall looking down. These hikes are very easy, less than a half mile in length, and are well marked for points like Sentinel Dome and Taft Point. Be careful though, as you can quickly emerge from a wooded area only to find you are very close to a nearly 4,000 foot drop off a cliff's edge!

There is food, souvenirs, and film available for purchase at Glacier Point. There are also bathrooms. Again, this overlook is not to be missed or skipped on any visit to Yosemite!

I feel compelled to explain something here: I realize this book is heavily weighted on hiking. Again, there is tremendous fun and relaxation to be had even for those who despise hiking. However, in keeping with the National Park credo to not overly disturb the natural beauty, roads and auto access is limited, in the sense that the most beautiful things are often only accessible via hiking trails. Fortunately for Yosemite, due to the valley cut by Mother Nature, highlights like Half Dome, El Capitan, and Yosemite and Bridalveil Falls are very easily viewed from places accessible by car. However, many other highlights, such as Illilouette, Vernal, and Nevada Falls, along with most of the Giant Sequoias, are only accessible by dusting off the hiking boots and getting to it!

Chapter 8

TOURS

Numerous tours are available. I strongly suggest visiting www.yosemitepark.com/activities for a much more complete list of tours than I will discuss here. There, you will also find information on bus tours originating from San Francisco, Fresno, and other locations outside of Yosemite.

Most all of the tours listed here require advance reservations, which can be made by calling 209-372-4FUN (4386) or from any Tour and Activity Desk or house phone within the park by calling extension 1240. Tour desk locations and hours are:

Yosemite Lodge Tour Desk	7:00 am – 9:00 pm (Mon. – Fri.)
	7:00 am – 7:00 pm (Sat. & Sun.)
Village Store Tour Kiosk	9:00 am – 6:00 pm
Curry Village Tour Kiosk	7:30 am – 6:00 pm
Big Trees Tour Kiosk	9:00 am – 5:00 pm

All offer reduced ticket prices for seniors, children, and complimentary tickets for kids under five years old when traveling with a paid adult. I will only list the full adult prices as of January 2009 under each tour.

Day tours from within the park include the Valley Floor Tour, the Glacier Point Tour, the Big Trees Tram Tour, the Glacier Point Stargazing Tour, the Valley Moonlight Tour, and the complete Grand Tour. The tour department also offers a Tuolumne Meadows hikers bus. Allow me to briefly discuss each tour.

The Yosemite Valley Floor Tour

This is a two-hour, ranger narrated, open-air tram tour, in summer. A heated motor coach is available late October through April. The tour takes you to see the major points in the valley. The tour leaves from the Yosemite Lodge, valley Shuttle Bus Stop #8, and takes you to see Yosemite Falls, Half Dome, El Capitan, Tunnel View, and Bridalveil Falls. Tickets cost $25 per adult.

Upper Yosemite Falls in Late July

The Glacier Point Tour

This is a four-hour round-trip tour from the valley to see Glacier Point. It operates late spring through early fall and stops at various valley sights, including Tunnel View and Glacier Point. It departs from in front of the Yosemite Lodge at the Falls at 8:30 am, 10:00 am, and 1:30 pm. Adult tickets are $41 round-trip. There is a $25 one-way ticket for hikers who wish to hike back down to the valley.

The Big Trees Tram Tour

This audio tour is in an open air tram, available May through October, and does not require advance reservations. However, reservations are still advised. It follows a paved road through the Lower and Upper Groves at Mariposa and stops at the Mariposa Log Cabin Museum. Cost is $25.50 for adults.

Galen Clark Tree, (upper) Mariposa Grove

The Glacier Point Stargazing Tour

This offers a guided bus tour to Glacier Point. It provides education on the natural history of the park; nighttime

75

views of Yosemite Falls, Nevada Falls, Vernal Falls, and Half Dome; as well as a one-hour astronomy program under the stars. It lasts about four hours and departs from in front of the Yosemite Lodge at the Falls. Tickets cost $41 per adult. You might want to bring a warm jacket and flashlight on this one.

The Yosemite Valley Moonlight Tour

This is basically the same tour as the Valley Floor Tour, only under the stars. The departure time for this two-hour tour varies with the time that the moon rises. The tour is offered on the four nights leading up to a full moon, as well as the night of the full moon, from late spring through early fall. The tour departs from in front of the Yosemite Lodge at the Falls, and tickets cost $25 for an adult.

The Tuolumne Meadows Hikers Bus

This bus departs from Curry Village at 8:00 am (Shuttle Bus Stop #13B), from the Fire House in Yosemite Village at 8:05 am (Shuttle Bus Stop #2), and from Yosemite Lodge at the Falls at 8:20 am (Shuttle Bus Stop #8). It is available from July through Labor Day only. For pick-up from the Ahwahnee Hotel, you must call 209-372-8441. Cost varies based upon where you are picked up from and where you are dropped off. Destinations include Olmsted Point, Tenaya Lake, Tuolumne Meadows, and other locations.

The Grand Tour

This magnificent all-day tour departs from in front of the Yosemite Lodge at the Falls at 8:45 am. You will visit multiple valley sights, Tunnel View, Glacier Point, Wawona, the Mariposa Grove, and more. You will also enjoy lunch in the famous Wawona Hotel Dining Room. Ticket prices are $92 ($82 without lunch) per adult.

Chapter 9

IMPORTANT PHONE NUMBERS & WEBSITES

EMERGENCY   911

General Information   209-372-0200
www.nps.gov/yose

General Activities Information
                             209-372-4FUN (4386)

Valley Visitor Center   209-372-0299
                             9:00 am – 7:00 pm,
                             Open Year-round

Tuolumne Meadows Visitor Center
                             209-372-0263
                             9:00 am – 6:00 pm,
                             Closed in Winter

Medical Clinic   209-372-4637, 8:00am–7:00pm
                             Drop-in 24-Hour Emergency

Dental Services   209-372-4200

Kennel   209-372-8348
                                8:00 am – 4:30 pm, Located at
                                the stable in the valley

Yosemite Guidebooks   209-379-2648
www.yosemitestore.com

Weather and road conditions / construction
                                209-372-0200
www.nps.gov/yose/planyourvisit/conditions.htm

Wilderness Permits   209-372-0740

Lodging Reservations   801-559-5000
www.yosemitepark.com

Lodging outside the park:
                                Highway 120 / Big Oak Flat –
                                West Entrance
                                Yosemite Chamber of Commerce
                                800-449-9120
                                209-962-0429

                                Tuolumne County Visitors Bureau
                                800-446-1333
                                www.thegreatunfenced.com

                                El Portal / Highway 140 / Arch Rock -
                                West Entrance
                                Yosemite Mariposa Tourism Bureau
                                866-425-3366
                                209-966-7081
                                www.homeofyosemite.com

Fish Camp / Oakhurst / Highway 41 / South Entrance
Yosemite Sierra Visitors Bureau
559-683-4636
www.yosemitethisyear.com

Lee Vining / Highway 120 / Tioga Pass - Northeast Entrance
Lee Vining Chamber of Commerce and Mono Lake Visitors Center
760-647-6629
www.leevining.com

Campgrounds   877-444-6777
www.recreation.gov

Badger Pass Ski Area   209-372-8430
www.badgerpass.com

Naturalist Activities – Yosemite Association
209-379-2321
www.nps.gov/yose/planyourvisit/things2do.htm

Stables, Mule and Horse Riding
209-372-8348, Valley (Shuttle Bus Stop #18)
7:00 am – 5:00 pm

209-375-6502, Wawona
7:00 am – 5:00 pm

Bike, Raft, & Ice Rink   Curry Village, 209-372-8319
hours vary

Bike Rental   Yosemite Lodge at the Falls
                               209-372-1208
                               hours vary

Yosemite Mountaineering School and Guide Services
Guided Climbing & Day Hikes
                               Curry Village, 209-372-8344
                               8:30 am – 12:00 pm, 1:00 pm –
                               5:00 pm

                               Tuolumne Meadows
                               209-372-8435
                               9:00 am – 6:00 pm

Tours – Open Air Tram in Summer, Enclosed Tour Bus
in Winter
                               209-372-4FUN (4386) or
                               209-372-1240
                               For any tour originating from
                               the valley,
                               (all tours except Mariposa Grove)

                               209-375-1621
                               9:00 am – 5:00 pm
                               Mariposa Grove Tour,
                               Summer Only
                               www.yosemitepark.com

Ahwahnee Hotel Dining Room
                               209-372-1489

The Mountain Room Restaurant
                               209-372-1281,   (reservations
                               accepted for parties of eight or
                               more only, 209-372-1274)

Wawona Hotel Dining Room
209-375-1425

Tuolumne Meadows Lodge Dining Room
209-372-8413

White Wolf Lodge   209-372-8416

Lost and Found

Hotels, Restaurants, Busses
209-372-4357

All Other Areas
209-379-1001

Yosemite Valley Chapel   209-372-4831
www.yosemitevalleychapel.org

Bear Sightings (Report)   209-372-0322

DNC Parks and Resorts at Yosemite
801-559-5000
www.yosemitepark.com

NOTE: Any hours of operation listed in this chapter should be considered peak summer season hours of operation.

Chapter 10

WHY IS A NATIONAL PARK VACATION ECONOMICAL?

Just in case you always thought of the national parks as an expensive trip or a vacation for the rich and famous, you will be pleased to learn that this is not the case. Let's get the expensive part out of the way first.

Unless you are one of the lucky ones who live within a reasonable drive of a major national park like Yosemite, you will have to purchase airfare and a rental car at the airport. These items are expensive; I agree. However, this is where the expensive part ends. Remember, as I stated earlier, your admission to the park is $20. That's all, for an entire week, and for your entire family.

Get out your calculator and start adding the cost for admission to a theme park, sporting event, etc. Be sure to budget for each member of your family and for each day. Getting kind of expensive isn't it? Now add in food.

Again, if you are a hiker, you are talking sub sandwiches with Subway® type prices for lunch on the trail everyday. Breakfast can be muffins and fruit from the grocery.

Oh, did I forget lodging? Book early, preferably a year early if you know what you wish to do because the demand for a room with a view, meaning any accommodation located in the heart of the Yosemite Valley, far exceeds supply. Peak-season rates vary from $179 for a standard room at the Yosemite Lodge at the Falls, to $140 for a cabin with a bath at Curry Village, to $92 for an unheated canvas tent cabin at Curry Village, to $79 for a "bring-your-own-linens" unit at Housekeeping Camp. Standard rooms at the fabulous AAA Four-Diamond Ahwahnee Hotel range from $443 peak-season to $408 off-season; higher priced featured rooms and suites are also available. Basic rule of thumb: accommodations with a private bathroom go first and fast. Compare that to what you normally spend for a room at a typical chain hotel along some highway you soon forgot!

Then there's the evening entertainment. Remember, there's a fantastic and free ranger program. Compare that to Cirque Du Soleil® ticket prices. Getting the picture? Other than getting there, this is the most economical way I can think of to spend a high quality week with your family.

Chapter 11

WILDLIFE IN YOSEMITE

As mentioned previously, wildlife is abundant at Yosemite. Always ask about both weather conditions and wildlife sightings. If you are lucky, you will see black bears, mule dear, coyotes, yellow-bellied marmots, pikas, and the beautiful blue stellar's jay. There are also mountain lions, peregrine falcons, California bats, great horned owls, grey fox, and porcupines within Yosemite. You might (but I doubt you will) also see rattlesnakes; not that you'd be lucky in this case. The wildlife at Yosemite or any national park is not to be feared, just respected and understood.

I have visited most of the great national parks in the United States and western Canada and have never had a bad or even close to dangerous experience with wildlife. First of all, even though there are estimates of five hundred black bears in Yosemite, it took me five visits until I saw one, and then I saw three within a twenty-four-hour period. There are no grizzly bears in Yosemite, and the species of black bear is not necessarily descriptive of the color. They may be golden, cinnamon, brown, or black in color. In any case, do not let the knowledge that there is wildlife running wild in a national park keep you from enjoying the park.

While I would not suggest petting a deer, most wildlife, including deer, will not even consider approaching humans, as long as you mind your business and let them go about theirs. Remember, this is their home, and you are the visitor here.

A park ranger at Jasper National Park in Alberta Canada once told the audience at a program I was attending that there was greater chance of getting killed by falling trees than by a bear. The only wildlife that under normal conditions might pose any risk to you are bears, mountain lions, and rattlesnakes. Even coyotes will not approach humans, unless it is a very small child left wandering alone. Be sure to keep small children close, especially on trails, and be prepared to pick them up.

In my five visits to Yosemite, I have never seen a rattlesnake or a mountain lion. They are both native to Yosemite, yet sightings of both are quite rare. The best, yet highly unlikely chance of encountering a rattlesnake is probably at the drier and milder Hetch Hetchy area. Both rattlesnakes and mountain lions are usually calm, quiet, and very elusive. Rattlesnakes make a hissing type sound. Their sound might also be described as similar to a baby's rattle; hence the name. Experts say rattlesnakes will not attack unless cornered or disturbed. However, they are known to defend themselves. If you do see one, keep your distance.

Bears are much the same and will probably not be seen if you make noise. When hiking or where your sight line might be impaired by trees or brush, especially if you might be down wind from an animal on trails, talk to yourself or others in your party, sing, carry a "bear bell" or loudly say, "Hello bear." If the animal knows you are nearing, they will instinctively go in another direction. These animals will only attack you if they feel threatened, cornered, have young with them, believe you want to harm them, or do not know you are there until you are right upon them. I have hiked in every park I've visited, including all over Glacier National Park, where the "WARNING BEAR COUNTRY" signs are posted everywhere.

Some people think I am a nerd, probably for more reasons than just the fact that I wear a bell, but it never hurts. It cost me $3.99 at a souvenir shop, many years ago, at Glacier National Park. I always look like the "dork" with my "bear bell". Be advised that there are some conflicting studies as to the effectiveness of bear bells. I hum, sing, and talk to myself, and have never had a problem. However, on the rare incidence where you do see a bear, it is important to know how to react.

If you find yourself too close to a black bear or mountain lion, make yourself bigger, and do not run or panic. Hold your arms up, stand tall, put children on your shoulders, and stand close together with others in your party. However, do not surround the animal; leave them a way to get away from you. Again, they should only be expected to attack if they feel cornered. The animal will see you as more intimidating and larger and will be less likely to think they can attack you and win the fight. Make noise, tell them to get away and back off slowly. Another good move is to throw rocks or dirt clods in the animal's direction as you back away.

Bears may bluff charge humans. If this happens, stand your ground, continue to make yourself look as large as you can, and let the bear back off. Then you should immediately do the same. Actual bear attacks are very rare. However, if indeed, despite all this, you are attacked, bear experts suggest curling up in a ball on the ground with your hands covering the back of your neck. This position will protect two of your most vulnerable areas, your stomach and your neck. However, if this does not work and the bear does not quickly stop and back off, bear experts say to fight back with all you've got!

If you can "bear" the facts (get it?), here are some: The National Park Service, Department of the Interior statistics show that there are approximately five hundred bear incidents at Yosemite in an average year. As of early December 2008, there was nearly $75,000 in property damage (year-to-date) attributed to bears at Yosemite. There were also more than twenty-five bears hit by cars. And don't think that the bears are only being seen or only doing property damage in some remote high country. They are coming to where the food is.

Where is food located? Food is located where the people are located! Also, where is expensive property located? Expensive property (automobiles, camper trailers, and RVs) is brought in by and kept with people! Vehicles are frequently broken into and damaged at the Yosemite Lodge at the Falls, the Ahwahnee, Curry Village, and throughout the Yosemite Village, as well as other very popular locations. A "bear incident" defines any time a bear causes a monetary loss to an individual, causes property damage, steals food, or injures a person.

You must take proper precautions with food. If day hiking, keep food very near to you and never leave it unattended. Don't turn your back on your food. If backpacking in the wilderness, you must store your food overnight in bear resistant food containers. You may have previously heard of hanging food suspended in air with a counterbalance; this method is no longer legal.

If you are staying in one of the various campgrounds, the Housekeeping Camp or the Curry Village Tent Cabins, you must use food lockers. Food Lockers are available at every campsite, housekeeping unit, and tent cabin. Also, treat your trash the same as your uneaten food. Store it in the same way, and do not leave it out.

If you are staying in a hotel, lodge room, or cabin, you must keep your food in the room overnight. If you are not in the room with it, you must keep windows and doors closed.

Do not leave food or other items with scent (which are therefore considered "food"), such as canned goods, soaps, cosmetics, drinks, or trash, in any vehicle overnight. You may only store food in your vehicle during daylight hours and with the windows closed and the items completely out of sight. There is a fine of up to $5,000 and possible impoundment of the vehicle for violation of this policy.

Now this may require a little thinking. If you are like me, I usually drive into Yosemite with a rental vehicle and a reservation at the Yosemite Lodge. I am not planning on overnight hiking or doing any camping. Therefore, I don't need to worry about violating this policy, right? Wrong!

If you took my advice and picked up maybe a twelve-pack of soft drinks and a bag of pretzels, or even brought a half-dozen energy bars from home for your hikes, you must remember to remove these from your vehicle after dark. If you purchased a single canned or bottled soft drink when you got gas and are used to leaving such items in the cup holder of your vehicle, don't do it here. You will be in violation and risk a huge fine! Be sure to remove candy wrappers or the mess your kids left in their seat. Take this policy and advice very literally. If you need a food locker, they are available at Curry Village parking lots and nearly all trailhead parking areas.

The bottom line here is that you must be "bear smart." A park ranger once told me that they have never recorded a human fatality at the hands of a bear in the history of Yosemite. Maybe that's true; maybe it's not. However, I do know that bears want nothing to do with humans. For example, if you are hiking down a trail in the vicinity of a bear and they hear or smell you coming, they will go another direction and you will never even know they were there. Again, it took me five visits to Yosemite to see a bear. Remember what they say, "You do not have to be able to outrun the bears, just the other campers!" Think about it!

The park requests that you report bear sightings to the Bear Management Team at 209-372-0322, or inform any park ranger.

Black Bear snacking on apples high in a tree, in the Yosemite Valley, near the base of Yosemite Falls.

Chapter 12

WHAT TO DO IF YOU ONLY HAVE ONE, TWO, OR THREE DAYS

The first thing to do if you only have one day to spend at this magical park is to sit down and have a good cry, pound the dash of your car, or look in the mirror and get really mad at yourself. Yosemite necessitates and deserves much more than one day to do it justice. I would compare this situation to taking your kids to Disney World for the first time and telling them after you enter the gate that they only have ten minutes to do it all.

Oh well, if you do indeed have just ONE DAY at Yosemite for your first visit, I would concentrate on the Yosemite Valley. There is more to do, and within close proximity, in the valley than anywhere else in the park. I would suggest beginning at the valley Visitor Center near the Yosemite Lodge. Here you can see a short movie detailing the main aspects of the park. You can also see interpretive displays and talk with a park ranger.

After this, I would suggest taking the Yosemite Valley Floor Tour. These are very well worth the cost of a ticket and are led and narrated by a very knowledgeable park employee. The tram (enclosed coach bus in winter) will also take you up to Tunnel View for an unbelievable look back at the entire valley.

If you are efficient with your time, this will still allow you time for a moderate hike. The Mist Trail, beginning at the trailhead at Happy Isles (Shuttle Bus Stop #16), in the far eastern part of the valley, will take you to both Vernal and Nevada Falls. This is, in my opinion, the most scenic part of the park and will leave you with the memory of an unbelievable hike.

You can then end your day with dinner at the Mountain Room Restaurant, behind the Yosemite Lodge at the Falls. You can also dine in the cafeteria, also behind the lodge. After dinner, you can end your one-day visit with the free ranger program at the outdoor amphitheatre, just outside these two restaurants.

If you only have TWO DAYS, I would add to the above a side trip to Glacier Point. This follows the Glacier Point Road and ends at an incredible overlook down to the valley. You might even consider hiking to Glacier Point via the four-mile trail. You can add to this a trip to see Giant Sequoias trees at either the Merced or Tuolumne Groves, located not far from the valley along the Big Oak Flat Road, Highway 120 northwest out of the valley. If hiking is more your idea of fun, there are a number of appealing trails in the valley or along the Glacier Point Road that you can choose from, including the very strenuous trail from the valley to the top of Upper Yosemite Fall or the relatively moderate Panorama Trail from Glacier Point. I would take it just half way (to save time) to see Illilouette Fall and then return to your vehicle at Glacier Point.

If you are fortunate enough to have THREE DAYS, then your possibilities are far less limited. While you can spend weeks and months at Yosemite, three days will give you a fairly broad experience. In addition to the suggestions above, you can consider a trip to Hetch Hetchy to the north or a trip south to see Wawona and the Mariposa Grove (located 35 miles south of the Yosemite Valley). The best suggestion for variety (provided you at least go to the Merced or Tuolumne Grove because you must see Giant Sequoia trees) would be to take Tioga Road north of the valley and into the high country to see a totally different Yosemite. Here, you will find none of the world's tallest waterfalls, no Giant Sequoias, and no world class hotel, but you will also encounter fewer numbers of tourists and have endless options of moderate hikes to see old mines, quaint lakes, historic rock domes, and more. You can get good and economical meals at Tuolumne Meadows or Crane Flat.

Chapter 13

ACTIVITIES JUST FOR THE KIDS

National parks, including Yosemite, are great places for kids to have fun. They will enjoy the various wildlife, old-fashioned campfires, interpretive displays at the visitor centers, and much more. There are wildlife exhibits at Happy Isles (shuttle bus stop #16), and children's programs, such as story time, games, and children's theatre. It is best to check the free park newspaper, or ask a ranger at the visitor's center for specifics.

The best activity for kids, in my opinion, is the Junior Ranger Program (similarly the Little Cubs Program for children between the ages of three and six) for kids seven to thirteen years of age. A self guided booklet is sold for $3.50 at the various visitors' centers throughout the park. Children can complete the booklet, requiring them to answer questions about plant life, wildlife, conservation in the park, responsibilities of park rangers, etc. It usually requires them to attend at least one evening ranger program and may also require a short hike or visits to certain places in the park. Upon completion, your child will be so proud and excited to be named a Junior

Ranger, with an oath sworn in by a park ranger. They will receive a certificate and badge (or patch). Yosemite alone swears in over 350,000 Junior Rangers each year.

My children are too old now, but through the years, they both became Junior Rangers at Denali, Grand Canyon (see photo), Yellowstone, Grand Teton, Crater Lake, Oregon Caves, Kenai Fjords, Redwood, and other national parks and national monuments.

Example of Junior Ranger Program Activity Booklet, Certificate, and Badge from Grand Canyon National Park. My kids were too young, and then too old, to participate on our visits to Yosemite.

Chapter 14

WEATHER, WINTER & SNOW CHAIN REQUIREMENTS

Weather, much like the black bear, is not a reason to avoid coming to Yosemite. It is yet another good reason to come. However, weather is something to pay close attention to and to always know what is forecasted to come.

Temperatures vary greatly by elevation, and therefore, by sections of the park. The high country along the Tioga Road and the highest elevations along the mountain ranges to the east and southeast are much colder than the Yosemite Valley or Hetch Hetchy areas.

Normal high temperatures for the valley range from the mid-80s to 90 degrees in the busiest months of July through September to a still very tolerable mid to upper 40s in the coldest months of December and January. Lows range from the low 50s in the summer to the mid-20s in the winter. Notice that very warm summer days usually turn into quite chilly evenings. The park can get very heavy snow in winter and can receive as much as fifty or more inches per month in December through April.

The park has about 50 percent cloudy days in winter but promises a 90 percent chance of a sunny day in summer. The greatest weather threat to safety is lightening on exposed, rocky peaks in summer. As mentioned previously, DO NOT be on exposed peaks, like Half Dome, when lightening or thunderstorms are present or forecasted.

Remember, Yosemite is open year-round. The Tioga Road and the high country are closed in winter, but the valley is open and winter activities in the valley as well as up at Badger Pass are awaiting you.

My wife and I once spent a week at Yosemite around the Thanksgiving Holiday. The weather was actually very accommodating for our plans to hike. Muddy trails were our main hindrance, not the temperatures. The key to activity during cooler periods is to dress in layers. We started out with a light shirt, covered by a heavier shirt, covered by a sweatshirt, and then a down vest. As the mornings turned into mid-day and the cardio-activity continued to give us a good workout, we kept pealing off layers until we were just hiking in long-sleeve t-shirts.

A consequence of cooler months is the possible short notice and arrival of snow. Federal regulations within Yosemite, as well as California state law which applies outside of the park, require snow chains or cables in snowy or icy road conditions. Weather and road conditions dictate when chains are required, and motorists are notified by the presence of signs that read "CHAINS REQUIRED."

It is not possible to determine for sure when conditions may require chains. Therefore, motorists are REQUIRED to carry chains in their vehicle November through May. DON'T ASK OR RELY ON CAR RENTAL COMPANIES! They do not know the rules, and quite frankly, they do not care. They are not concerned with where you are taking the rental car once you rent it at some airport. They just want your money.

I once rented a vehicle and made sure when I reserved it that it would have chains in it. When I picked up the car at the airport, I was assured the chains were in the trunk. However, I made the mistake of not checking. I did check as I got close to Yosemite and found there were no chains anywhere in the vehicle. Lucky for me (and it was just dumb luck), I found an auto parts store that sold me a set, (over $50) with the very kind offer that if I did not need them (meaning that if I did not open the package) I could return them for a full refund. Well, I was lucky. We did not need them, and I did return them on my way back to the airport.

Again, law requires chains during half the year so that if they have to post the "CHAINS REQUIRED" signs, everyone can simply pull over and attach the chains they are carrying with them. These signs will tell you if your vehicle is exempt (four-wheel drive or snow tires, for example) and are posted where it is relatively safe to pull over and put them on or near turnouts that can be used for such purpose. Failure to put on chains where required is subject to a fine up to $5,000. Plus, you may be required to park your vehicle and call for a tow service to either tow the car or bring out chains. Imagine how much additional this would cost you? "Chains required" signs have been posted as early as September and as late as May! Finally, the speed limit in chain control areas is 25 mph, regardless of whether higher speed limit signs are still up.

Usually (and I say usually because there are always exceptions due to weather), the Wawona Road (Highway 41 from Fresno), the Big Oak Flat Road (Highway 120 from Manteca), the El Portal Road (Highway 140 from Merced), and the Hetch Hetchy Road (8:00 am to 5:00 pm) are open year-round. The five mile section of the Glacier Point Road providing access up to Badger Pass is plowed mid December through March. Otherwise, from sometime in November through late May or early June, it is closed along with the rest of Glacier Point Road.

You should expect the Mariposa Grove Road to be closed late November or early December through mid April. Glacier Point Road (beyond Badger Pass) and the Tioga Road are closed from sometime in November through late May or early June.

As far as lodging, the Ahwahnee and the Yosemite Lodge at the Falls are open year-round. Curry Village and the Wawona are unpredictable, and I highly suggest calling first. Both are usually open select weekends in the colder months. Housekeeping Camp, Tuolumne Meadows Lodge, and White Wolf Lodge are closed in the colder months. Remember reservations are accepted 366 days (one year plus one day) in advance.

Campgrounds also vary, with certain ones open year-round and others open seasonally. I checked in February of 2009, and Upper Pines and Camp 4 in the valley were open on a first-come basis. The North and Lower Pines were closed for the season. Serving other parts of the park, Hodgdon Meadow and Wawona Campgrounds were open on a first-come basis while Porcupine Flat, Crane Flat, Tamarack Flat, Yosemite Creek, White Wolf, and Bridalveil Creek Campgrounds were closed for the season.

Again, as of February 2009, all valley based trails were open, except sections of the Mist, John Muir, and Four Mile trails. Also, as to be expected, the Half Dome Cables were down for the season. They are usually reinstalled just before the third weekend in May. Another tip here: I hate the way the park words it when they say that the Half Dome Cables are down seasonally. What I would like them to say is, "The cables are down, and therefore, THE HALF-DOME TRAIL

IS CLOSED." DO NOT try to climb Half-Dome without the cables. There are fools out there who try this. Please, do not be one of them!

Chapter 15

WILDFIRES

Fires are regular occurrences in any large forest, and in fact, occur in any large national park during the hot and dry periods of the year. They are a necessary and an integral part of creating the beauty and landscape. Yes, of course, you do not want to be caught in a fire. You need to be aware of any fires in the area and the fire hazard level, and you must practice fire precautions. However, fire is nature's way of clearing old and dead growth and creating room for new seedlings to sprout and grow.

Years ago, the National Park Service had vastly different protocols for dealing with fire in the parks. They used to do everything in their power to put out fires as quickly as possible. Today, most are allowed to burn under a watchful professional eye, making exceptions to keep them from getting too large and to protect historical buildings and sites in the parks. After decades of the Park Service doing all it could to suppress fire, they eventually realized that allowing naturally occurring fires to burn thins the forests and allows the canopy overhead to open and the needed sunlight to reach lower into the forest.

Fire suppression eventually leads to such a huge build-up of dead and dry timber and bush that eventually lightening or a careless camper will ignite a fire that can grow to horrific and historic levels. This creates a much greater threat to the parks, its wildlife, and humans. Have you heard the term "prescribed fires" or "controlled burn?" This refers to the practice of fire professionals intentionally creating fires in sections of a park to eliminate the build-up of dead timber and undergrowth, which can greatly intensify wildfires. This keeps the danger of a huge or catastrophic fire at a relatively low level.

A process called "mechanical thinning" is also used at Yosemite. This process is basically using chain saws to remove certain vegetation, often smaller and less desirable trees, to lessen the chance of fire and to provide safer conditions and better access for firefighters.

In addition, national parks used to believe that fire was a major contributing factor to the decline in the number of Giant Sequoias. They scrambled to immediately douse fires in these forests because these large and historic trees are becoming fewer and fewer, and as is true today, a park priority is doing all that is humanly possible to save and protect them. However, through the years, they came to realize that this protocol, of not allowing the natural process, led to the buildup of layers and layers of dead brush, prohibiting the seedlings from ever reaching soil to sprout new trees, and ironically, was contributing to the reduction of Giant Sequoias.

Besides, the Giant Sequoia is naturally fire resistant. The bark is fire resistant, and the branches are so high up that they are usually too high for flames to reach. The fire clears the brush to allow a path to the soil below, and the heat is an important element in opening up the cones and scattering the tiny seeds. This is truly a prime example of what is referred top as a "fire adapted species."

A prime example of the extensive fire loss that can occur if the buildup of dead forest and underbrush is allowed to accumulate, combined with an equally critical practice of setting limits as to how large to let a natural fire grow to before taking swift action to suppress it's further growth, are the historic Yellowstone fires of 1988. These fires burned 793,000 acres within Yellowstone National Park, over 1.2 million acres ecosystem wide, and nearly destroyed the historic and irreplaceable Old Faithful Inn. Thank goodness that the highly skilled firefighters were able to save the inn.

In the years since, the forests have made a remarkable recovery on their own due to Mother Nature's fine work. The park service, in analyzing the fire in retrospect and in harvesting all that could be learned from the event, made policy changes. As a result, they no longer put out all the smaller fires that occur naturally. They came to understand that this activity, combined with greater than normal rainfall, had greatly assisted in creating the huge fire source that was just waiting to be ignited. Unfortunately, mother nature ignited a historic fire in 1988.

Chapter 16

YOSEMITE'S NEIGHBORING, MAJESTIC NATIONAL PARKS

It should not come as news to anyone that there are many additional sites to see in California, and within close proximity to Yosemite National Park. To the east are Mono Lake, Devil's Postpile National Monument, and Mammoth Mountain Ski Area. To the north are Reno, Nevada, and Lake Tahoe. A half hour drive to the south is beautiful Bass Lake, where much of the movie *The Great Outdoors* was filmed.

Here, I want to share a few thoughts on the majestic, yet totally overshadowed by Yosemite, sister national parks of Sequoia and Kings Canyon. They are located just to the southeast of Yosemite, along the Sierra Nevada Range.

These fantastic national parks are also very easily reached from a trip originating with a flight into the Fresno Airport. They are jewels in their own right and easily justify a trip all their own. However, if you have extra time on your tip to Yosemite, read on. If you fear that you will never be in this part of the country again, you'll want to be able to say that you have been to Sequoia and Kings Canyon National Parks.

Sequoia and Kings Canyon go together like Minneapolis goes with Saint Paul, or Dallas goes with Fort Worth. To make a more appropriate national park analogy, they go together like Yellowstone and Grand Teton National Parks. They are inseparable. At the same time, they are also very different.

My wife and I devoted a summer's vacation to these two wonderful parks, and we are so very glad we did.

The drive east, out Highway 180 from Fresno, is like the drive to Yosemite. It is quite beautiful in its own way, as it quickly turns from flat and desert-like to hilly, then mountainous and green. It will take you about two hours from the Fresno airport (53 miles).

Having mentioned earlier that Yosemite was our country's third national park, Sequoia was the second, and Yellowstone was the first. Sequoia became a national park on September 25, 1890, via the bill signed by President Benjamin Harrison. Sequoia has the greatest concentration of Giant Sequoia trees anywhere in the world. The typical tree here is not bigger or better than the typical tree in Yosemite's Mariposa Grove. It's just that there are many more, and continuous grove after grove to see, drive, and hike through. Of the fifty-seven known groves of Giant Sequoias on earth, thirty of them are in these two parks. The Giant Forest Grove in Sequoia National Park has an estimated 10,657 Giant Sequoia trees alone.

Sequoia National Park features the General Sherman tree, thought to be the largest living tree, and largest living thing, in the world. The Giant Forest Grove also features the Washington Tree. It was once the world's second largest tree at over 246 feet tall, but since 2003 has lost much of its trunk, and therefore, its ranking.

The park also features Crystal Cave, which you can explore, as well as Mount Whitney at its eastern border. Mount Whitney, at 14,494 feet, is the tallest mountain in the lower forty-eight states. Sequoia National Park has over one hundred caves and over 2,600 lakes and ponds.

Kings Canyon National Park's southern border is also the northern border of Sequoia National Park. Kings Canyon features a more desert-like climate and topography. It has a beautiful U-shaped canyon, formed like the Yosemite Valley was, from glaciers. The park has plenty of Giant Sequoia trees of its own and features the General Grant tree, the world's third largest tree.

Kings Canyon was the first park where my wife and I ever ran into a bear. We saw a large black bear, maybe fifty to seventy-five yards ahead of us while out on a day hike. We did as we had been advised and had no problem. Remember to always make noise when hiking, and DO NOT PANIC if you do see a bear! By doing so, we saw the bear well before we got too close to it. We simply scared it off by throwing dirt clods in its general direction and standing close together to appear as one large object.

Also, be aware that Kings Canyon has a larger population of snakes than Yosemite or even Sequoia, due to the arid, hot climate. Keep your eyes open. If you are bitten, remember to stay still and send for help (one of the many reasons to resist hiking alone). Bites are rarely fatal, but they need prompt and trained medical attention, and movement will spread the venom much more rapidly.

Much of both of these parks is total wilderness. A large percentage of Yosemite is wilderness, yet nothing compared to Sequoia and Kings Canyon. There is a spot in Sequoia that one can hike to where you will technically be further from a road or highway than any other place in the contiguous forty-eight states! You can walk (1/4th mile, 400 steps) to the top of Moro Rock, a large granite dome with an unparalleled view of the Great Western Divide.

Also, and the park will downplay this, I have read of armed bandits who secretly grow marijuana within the Sequoia National Park boundary. Again, due to its wilderness and many highly secluded areas, this is possible. This is not to be feared unless you plan to hike many miles into the wilderness off of the well used, well marked, and well publicized trails. The criminals know where the secluded parts are, where they have very little chance of running into tourists. Remember, these particular national parks encompass extremely large land areas. Sequoia and Kings Canyon total more than 863,000 acres!

Both Sequoia and Kings Canyon feature full services like Yosemite: lodging, food, gas, and emergency help. A large portion of Sequoia National Park is open year-round. Both parks are officially open year-round; however, the road through Kings Canyon is only open in summer. Also, the main road in Sequoia National Park is the road between Lodgepole and Grant Grove. It is open year-round, but be prepared for temporary closure due to winter snows.

Activities are varied, and for the most part, very similar to Yosemite, with hiking, fishing, horseback riding, camping, majestic wildlife, ranger programs, etc. However, while similar in these arenas, every national park is unique. I find all of them well worth visiting.

For additional information on both Sequoia and Kings Canyon, call general park information at 559-565-3134, or lodging reservations at 888-252-5757 for Sequoia NP or 866-522-6966 for Kings Canyon NP.

Chapter 17

FINAL THOUGHTS

It just happens to be January 20, 2009, and I have come to the point where I need to gather my thoughts and figure out how I want to conclude this book. As I take a break from writing and re-tune into the endless day of presidential inauguration activities on the television, there it is. The networks are covering the luncheon for the new president, and California Senator Dianne Feinstein is basically the emcee for the events of the day, including the luncheon.

She asks President Obama, his cabinet and staff appointees, and all former presidents and other invited guests to focus their attention on the painting on the wall next to her. Right there on the wall, in Statuary Hall, in our nation's Capital Building, is the Yosemite Valley. The painting is the work of famous Yosemite painter Thomas Hill, and it commemorates President Lincoln's signing, in 1864, of the Yosemite Grant (Hills' studio is today on the grounds of the Wawona Hotel and serves as a National Park Service Visitors Center). There, in this beautiful work of art, is Half Dome, El Capitan, Bridalveil Fall, and the rest of this unbelievable park. It was a gift to President Theodore Roosevelt during his four-day visit to Yosemite to camp with naturalist John Muir.

Yosemite is like falling in love, riding a bike, or having a child. Visiting at least once is one of the items that should be on the short list of things you must do in your lifetime. Yosemite is such a breathtaking and valuable piece of our country that it gets prime visibility even at a presidential inauguration. I'd say that says it best.

John Muir once said, "No temple made with hands can compare with Yosemite." Well said, John! Come see, come enjoy, come experience, come bring your father to Yosemite like I did, and come figure out why you never came here before. Or, if you are one of the lucky ones, like your author, come return to Yosemite!

Appendix A

MISSELLANEOUS NATIONAL PARK TIPS

Book early! Book your trip, and especially your lodging as far in advance as possible, preferably six to twelve months. Due to limited availability and very reasonable pricing, cabins and other accommodations within the national parks rarely display a "vacancy" sign. Do not be under the misperception that there are chain motels within U.S. National Parks or that the lodging just outside the parks is convenient. Driving two or more hours round-trip to a hotel located outside the park will take much of the fun out of your trip. Book early. Ask questions about proximity to the main attractions, and have an unbelievable experience.

Stay in the park, if at all possible. It is part of the park experience to awaken in the park and walk out your cabin door to see the waterfalls or wildlife. Staying at a chain hotel is something you do when going to the beach or an amusement park, not a national park!

Consider taking your trip in the off-season. Parks are most crowded in the summer; still nothing compares to the crowds at other types of vacation destinations. However, if you travel in the fall or spring, you will have a much more relaxed time. Because of lessened crowds, you will see more wildlife. Also, you should not have to wait for a table at dinner. Finally, you will see stronger flowing waterfalls in spring or unbelievable fall color—and you will save money!

Attend as many evening ranger programs as possible. They are free, very informative, relaxing, and appropriate for the entire family. Besides, what else are you going to be doing without television or radio? That's right: most parks do not receive television or radio signals.

Take a deck of cards. While it is common to turn in early, due to all the exercise of walking or hiking during the day plus the relaxing effect of the fresh park air, you still need to occupy the early evening. Basically, you have two options for entertainment: attend the before mentioned ranger programs or bring your own entertainment.

Stop prior to entering the National Park and purchase snacks. You can find soft drinks and snacks within the parks, but often the general stores there have higher prices, close early, and offer a limited selection. Stopping in the last town or at the last gas/food mart will be a move you will be glad you made.

Never hike without water and food. You can always spot the novice (been there, done that). They are the ones three miles down a trail, sweating profusely, carrying a warm twelve-ounce plastic bottle of spring water, and asking questions like, "How much further do I have to go?" Why risk your life—or even not getting the most enjoyment out of a hike—by not being prepared? There is nothing macho about proving you can do a trail without refreshment. You need to get a backpack of some sort and have sufficient water (preferably cold, as with a CamelBak®) and food (at least energy bars, if not a sandwich). Remember, you only paid around $20 to get your entire family into the park for a full seven days. You certainly have enough money left for a backpack!

Heed the advice on wildlife. If you do, you'll be fine and have experiences you'll treasure for a lifetime. You have very little to fear if you use common sense. First of all, you may not see a bear. Second, if you do, they are more afraid of you than you are of them. If you keep your distance and learn what to do if one should come toward you, you'll be fine.

I will never forget two things I have been told that really taught me the ins and outs of wildlife. At Yellowstone, a ranger told me about the German tourist who asked his wife to take his picture while he put his arm around a bison. STUPID right? It killed him. At Jasper NP in Alberta Canada, a ranger stated that there have been more tourists killed by falling trees than by bears. In other words, be informed, act accordingly, and enjoy the kind of fabulous trip that only the national parks can provide.

Money saving tips: Eat breakfast in your room or cabin. You can get milk, juice, fruit, and pastries in the general store. This way, you only pay for two meals out each day. Not to confuse anyone here: food at national parks is cheap compared to the usual vacation destinations. Do not expect to set aside a Disney World type budget for this trip. At the same time, while most meals are very reasonable, it always pays to inquire ahead.

For example, at Yosemite, the famous and breathtaking Ahwahnee Hotel has a dining room that is not to miss.

However, prices here are slightly higher than most other parks' best dining, and higher than other options in Yosemite. Also, the dining room has a "resort casual" dress code for dinner. Resort casual means collared shirts and long pants for men, and dresses, skirts / slacks and blouses, or evening pants suits for women that will probably not be used at any other time on the trip. Who wants to have to pack a required outfit with limited suitcase space and airlines charging for each piece of checked baggage? Why not plan to have breakfast or lunch in the dining room? It is much cheaper. You can easily get in without a reservation, and it will allow you to experience eating in the same historic dining room.

Buy a photo album at a gift store within the park that has the name of the park on the outside. You will need to buy one anyway. Also, take a picture of your family by the park entrance sign. Every national park has a cool sign at each entrance, which makes for the ideal first photo in your picture album.

Buy your film, digital camera photo card, batteries, and an extra set of batteries at home. They may not have exactly what you need at the park, and even if they do, you will pay the captive audience pricing.

DAY HIKING ESSENTIALS

You need someone to hike with. Resist, if possible, the urge to hike alone.

Back Pack

CamelBak® and Water: Carry at least 150 percent of what you think you'll need. A CamelBak® maintains ice in your water for hours.

Food: Carry more than you think you'll need, and more than just lunch.
   *Sandwich: Keep the sandwich dry until the time you actually eat it. Add condiments when ready to eat.
   *Salty items: Nuts and chips, Pringles® carry especially well due to container protecting them from getting crushed.
   *Fruit
   *Energy bars, like Powerbar®

Trail Map

Hiking Boots

Thick Socks: Prevent those nasty blisters.

Compact Binoculars

Compass

Hat

Sunscreen

Insect Repellant

Bear Bell: This is almost always a good idea and is highly recommended at Yosemite, Rocky Mountain, Sequoia, Kings Canyon, Yellowstone, Grand Teton, Smoky Mountain, and a MUST at Glacier and all Alaska NPs.

Camera: Carry a disposable on the more challenging hikes. It's lighter, and there's no risk of breaking a good camera due to tough trails or late day fatigue.

Cell Phone: Do not rely on coverage.

Understanding Your Trail: How difficult is the rating? How much time does it normally take to complete? Are there any facilities along the way? How many hours of daylight do you have left?

Understanding the Weather Forecast: You do not want to be on exposed and high rock during l i g h t e n i n g. Also, you will need to understand the temperature expectations for differing times of the day. During certain times of the year, especially spring and fall, you will want to layer clothing. This will allow you to keep warm in the colder morning and evening periods, yet allow you to shed layers during the relatively warmer midday!

Hiking Permit: This is not usually required for day hiking, but it is the norm for overnight hiking.

Flashlight

Rain Gear

Finally, I wish to thank the National Park Service and Yosemite National Park for some of the absolute best family vacations, best moments, best days, and best memories of my entire life!

INDEX

Activities – *see also specific activities*
    Backcountry ski tours 51
    Bike rental 51, 79
    Bird watching 51
    Cross-country skiing 51
    Downhill skiing 51, 61
    Fishing 51, 62, 110
    Golfing 51
    Group hiking 51
    Hiking 4, 7–10, 12, 23, 36, 47, 51–53, 62, 64, 69–70, 86, 88–90, 92, 98, 109–110, 114
    Horseback riding 29, 51, 110
    Ice skating 51
    Photography 51, 55
    Ranger programs, evening 110, 114
    Rock climbing 51, 54, 58, 62
    Rock climbing lessons 51
    Shopping 51
    Sledding 51
    Snowboarding 51, 61

    Snowshoeing 51
    Swimming 11, 44, 49, 51, 62, 67
    Wading 51
Admission fees 83
Ahwahnee Hotel, the 11–12, 15, 17–18, 21, 24, 26, 28, 53, 55,
68, 76, 80, 84, 115
Amphitheaters 60
    Curry Village 60
    Lower Pines Campground 60
    Yosemite Lodge at the Falls 60
Ansel Adams Art Gallery 53
Backcountry ski tours 51
Bass Lake 107
Big Oak Flat entrance 49, 63, 65
Biking, bike rentals 79
Bears/bear sighting reporting 9, 81
Bighorn Sheep 62
Bird Watching 51
Box lunches 14
Camp 4 kiosk 59
Campgrounds 19, 79, 88, 100
    Bridalveil Creek 19, 100
    Camp 4 19, 100
    Crane Flat 19, 41, 100
    Hetch Hetchy 19
    Hodgdon Meadow 19, 100
    Lower Pines 19, 60, 100
    North Pines 19
    Porcupine Flat 19, 100
    Tamarack Flat 19, 100
    Tuolumne Meadows 19, 42, 100
    Upper Pines 19, 100
    Wawona 19, 60, 100

    White Wolf 19, 100
    Yosemite Creek 19, 100
Camp Mather 49, 63
Chapel, the Yosemite Valley 81
Children's activities 95, 96
Clouds Rest 44
Coyotes xvii, 85
Cross-country skiing 51
Crystal Cave 109
Curry Pavilion, the 11
Curry Village Coffee & Ice Cream Corner, the 11
Curry Village Ice Rink, the 51
Curry Village Pizza Deck & Bar, the 11
Degnan's Café 11
Degnan's Deli 11
Dental Services 77
Downhill skiing 51, 61
Dress Code 12–13, 18, 116
El Capitan xvii, 36, 52, 54, 58, 70, 72, 111
El Portal 8, 21, 23, 78, 99
Emerald Pool 32
Fish Camp 8, 21, 23, 78
Fishing 51, 62, 110
Food – *see also specific restaurants and food vendors* food xv, xvi, 8–9, 11–14, 30, 38, 59, 63, 70, 83, 88–89, 110, 114–115, 117
Food lockers 89
Fresno 1–2, 71, 99, 107, 108
Gas 2, 12, 61, 89, 110, 114
General Grant Tree 109
General Sherman Tree 108
Giant Forest 108

Giant Sequoias 48–49, 62, 64–65, 70, 92–93, 104, 108
Glacier Point 12, 28, 30–32, 35, 52–53, 60–61, 68–70, 72, 74–76, 92, 99, 100
Glacier Point Snack Stand, the 12
Grizzly Giant, the 46–47
Grove Museum, the 46, 66
Golden Crown Mine 44
Golf 12, 47, 51, 65, 67
Golf Pro Shop, the 12
Group hiking 51
Half Dome 10, 30–32, 36–40, 61, 68, 70, 72, 76, 98, 100–101, 111
Half Dome cables 37–40, 100
Happy Isles Nature Center, the 54–55
Happy Isles Snack Stand, the 11
Hetch Hetchy Reservoir 49–50, 64
Hiking xv, xvii, xviii, 4, 7–10, 12, 23, 27, 36, 47, 49, 51–53, 62, 64, 69–70, 86, 88–90, 92, 98, 109–110, 114, 117, 119
Hiking Trails 7, 23, 62, 70
    Bridalveil Fall, base of 28, 52
    Cathedral Lake 42
    Chilnualna Falls 46, 52–53
    Elizabeth Lake 42
    Gaylor and Granite Lakes 44
    Glacier Point 28, 30–32, 35, 52, 69
    Glen Aulin 43
    Half Dome 10, 30–32, 36–40, 61, 68, 70, 72, 76, 98, 100–101, 111
    High Sierra Loop 27
    John Muir Trail 27, 32, 35, 68
    Lembert Dome 41
    Lower Yosemite Fall, base of 28
    Mariposa Grove, lower 46
    Mariposa Grove, upper 46

    May Lake 43
    Merced Grove 49, 64–65
    Mist Trail 29–32, 35–36, 52–53, 68–69
    Mirror Lake 28
    Mono Pass 44
    Panorama Trail 30, 32, 35–36, 52–53, 68
    Sunrise Lakes 44
    Tuolumne Grove 49, 64–65
    Upper Yosemite Fall 29
    Wapama Falls 49, 52
History, park 24, 54, 65–66, 75, 90
Horseback riding 29, 51, 110
Ice Skating 51
John Muir 27, 30, 32, 35, 68, 100, 112
Junior Ranger Program 95–96
Kennel 77
Kings Canyon National Park 107, 109
LaConte Memorial Lodge 53, 55
Lee Vining 8, 23, 63, 79
Little Cubs Program 95
Little Yosemite Valley 37
Lodging 14, 17–18, 62, 78, 84, 100, 110, 113
Lost and Found 80
Mariposa Grove, the 21, 46, 48, 61, 65–66, 76, 93, 100
Medical clinic, the Yosemite 59
Merced Grove, the 49, 64–65
Merced River 29, 51–52, 68
Mono Craters 63
Mono Lake 44, 63, 79, 107
Moro Rock 110
Mount Whitney 109
Mountain Lions 85–86
Mountain Room Restaurant, the 11, 13, 80

Mountain Room Lounge, the 11
Mountain Shop at Curry Village, the 51
Mountaineering School, the Yosemite 79
Mule Dear 85
Oakhurst 2
Olmstead Point 62, 76
O'Shaughnessy Dam, the 63
Peregrine Falcon 59, 85
Phone numbers 23, 77
Photography 51, 55
Pioneer Yosemite History Center, the 51, 65, 67
Prescribed Burns 104
Raft rental 79,
Ranger talks/programs 60, 110, 114
Rattlesnakes 85–86
Redwoods, the 18
Road conditions 78, 98
Rock climbing xviii, 51, 54, 58, 62
Rock climbing lessons 51
Sequoia National Park 66, 108, 109, 110
Shopping 51
Shuttle bus, the valley 28–32, 38, 55, 72, 76, 79, 92, 95
Sierra Ghost Mine 44
Ski Buffet, the 14
Sledding 51
Sliders Grab-N-Go 12
Snow chains 98
Snow Skiing xvi, 51
Snowboarding 51, 61
Snowshoeing 51
Soda Springs 43
Stables 79
Swimming xvi, 11, 32, 44, 49, 51, 62, 67

Taqueria, the 14
Tenaya Canyon 44
Tenaya Lodge, the 21, 23
Thomas Hill 67, 111
Thomas Hill Studio, the 67
Tioga Pass 3, 42–44, 63, 79
Tioga Pass entrance 3, 42–44
Tioga Road 17, 27, 41–45, 49, 61–62, 65, 93
Tioga Road, the 41–45, 51, 97–98, 100
Tours
    Big Trees Tram Tour, the 71–72, 74
    Glacier Point Tour, the 69, 72, 74
    Glacier Point Stargazing Tour, the 72, 75
    Grand Tour, the 72, 76
    Yosemite Valley Floor Tour, the 72, 91
    Yosemite Valley Moonlight Tour, the 76
    Tuolumne Meadows Hikers Bus, the 72, 76
Tunnel View 72, 74, 76, 92
Tuolumne Grove, the 49, 65
Tuolumne Meadows Grill, the 12
Tuolumne Meadows Lodge, the 12, 14, 17–18, 80, 100
Tuolumne Meadows Stable, the 62
Tuolumne Meadows Visitor Center, the 61–62, 77
Valley Wilderness Center, the 53
Village Grill, the 11
Wading 51
Washington Tree 108
Waterfalls 7, 52, 62–63, 93, 113–114
    Bridalveil Fall 28, 52
    Chilnualna Falls 46, 52
    Horsetail Fall 52
    Illilouette Fall 52
    Nevada Fall 52

Ribbon Fall 52
Sentinel Falls 52
Tuolumne Falls 42
Vernal Fall 52
Wapama Falls 52
Yosemite Falls 28, 52
Wawona Hotel, the 12, 17, 65, 67, 111
Wawona Hotel Dining Room, the 12–13, 76, 80
Wawona Hotel Lawn Barbeque, the 12
Wawona Point overlook 46–47
Weather viii, 78, 85, 97–99, 118
White Wolf Lodge, the 12, 14, 17–18, 80, 100
White Cascade 43
Wilderness Permits 59, 78
Wildfires viii, 103–104
Wildlife viii, xiii, xvi–xviii, 7, 29, 54–55, 60, 85–86, 95, 104, 110, 113–115
Winter viii, 8, 12, 14, 51, 60, 61, 67, 69, 77, 80, 92, 97–99, 101, 110
Yellow-Bellied Marmots 62, 85
Yosemite Fund 32
Yosemite Lodge at the Falls, the 11, 13, 17–18, 60, 74, 76, 84, 88, 92, 100, 122
Yosemite Lodge Cone Stand, the 11
Yosemite Cemetery, the 53–54
Yosemite Museum, the 53–54, 58
Yosemite Theater, the 53
Yosemite Valley Visitor Center, the 54